GOOD LYRICS
make
GREAT POETRY

DR. JAMES R. MURPHY

1st WORLD
PUBLISHING

GOOD LYRICS make GREAT POETRY

DR. JAMES R. MURPHY

© Dr. James R. Murphy, 2005

Published by 1stWorld Publishing
1100 North 4th St. Suite 131, Fairfield, Iowa 52556
tel: 641-209-5000 • fax: 641-209-3001
web: www.1stworldpublishing.com

First Edition

ISBN: 1-59540-939-4
eBook ISBN: 1-59540-944-0
Library of Congress Catalog Number 2005925599

This material has been written and published solely for educational purposes. The author and the publisher shall have neither liability or responsibility to any person or entity with respect to any loss, damage or injury caused or alleged to be caused directly or indirectly by the information contained in this book.

The characters and events described in this text are intended to entertain and teach rather than present an exact factual history of real people or events.

Table of Contents

Lyrics from Truck Stop

Lyrics from Luke and Sarah

Lyrics from High School Daze

A TREE IS GOOD

A tree is good for many reasons
Giving wood and showing seasons
Come on neighbor, it's no crime
If kids think your tree's good to climb

QUEEN OF HEARTS

You smiled across the table and you said I got a pair
My dear you knew I knew it 'cause I couldn't help but stare
Of course you were referrin' to the cards there in your hand
You knew you'd get a raise from me 'cause I'm a bettin' man

It was written in the cards—you were mistress of the arts
The lady I was dealin' was the Queen of Hearts

You opened up and let me in and made me feel so good
I knew somehow we both'd win and that you understood
Sure enough, you called my bluff and nearly blew my mind
You said take care—a pair can soon become three of a kind

You surely were an actress and you really knew your parts
The lady I was dealin' was the Queen of Hearts

Well, that was many years ago when first you made me blush
You made me feel just like a king with a regal royal flush
Hear the beat of little feet runnin' all around the deck
I got myself a full house now—I think I better check

You were stacked and the deck was stacked
        and you had all the smarts
The lady I was dealin' was the Queen of Hearts

LEAVE A MESSAGE AT THE TONE

I Just tried to reach you on the phone again
I'm about to give up, that was number ten
Got the same old story from your telephone
I'm not here, please leave a message at the tone

Know I hurt your feelings, but I truly care
How can I apologize if you're not there
I'm so very sorry and I'm oh so all alone
Please don't say to leave a message at the tone

      I've told your tape recorder I am on my knees
      At least a hundred times I've begged you call me please
      Told you that I've loved you dear since don't know when
      And then I hear that damn depressing tone again

How can you be spiteful knowing how I've tried
You must feel delightful at the way I've cried
I feel like a fool and by now you should have known
If you want me, leave a message at the tone

MY YEARLY BALLOON

When I was a boy, I never had a toy
We were poor, but it really didn't matter
Whenever we butchered, I'd jump for joy
'Cause my yearly balloon was a bladder

HUMMINGBIRD

Scarlet throat, coat attractive
Must she be so hyper-active
Little creature God created
With the daffodils He mated
Lance for tool, look, no hands
As a rule, she never lands
Fact is that her task's so grueling
Must have air-to-air refueling
Winglets waiting, she must race
Hoverin' at a fast-food place
Tiny zephyr, so exotic
Nectar is a nice narcotic
Maybe pollen's her prescription
Magic acts defy description
It's astonishing the ease
With which she fools Mistopheles
Dancing, lancing, it's a fact
There's no cat can catch her act

POOR PAPA, POOR MAMA, POOR ME

Poor Papa was a bully, and the meanest man in town
And when he as a'drinkin', he could put the devil down
'Twas the devil in the bottle that made Papa lose his mind
His kids were always bloody 'cause he was the beatin' kind

> Poor Mama, poor Mama
> You will always be alone
> You'll never have another man
> That you can call your own

Poor Papa threw away his belt, and grabbed a two-by-two
He said you better shut up if you know what's good for you
I was beggin' and a'cryin' when it crashed into my head
Papa, don't hit little sister, please hit me again instead

> Poor Mama, poor Mama
> Your eyes went kinda wild
> You said I'll fix it
> You will never beat another child

Poor Papa raised the club again to give another whack
He never saw the pistol Mama held behind her back
She raised the gun up slowly and she carefully took aim
I cried Mama please don't do it 'cause I'm sure I am to blame

    Poor Mama, poor Mama
    Through the screamin' and the cries
    You pulled the trigger then and'
    Got him clean between the eyes

Poor Papa, poor Mama, poor me

THANK YOU FOR THE PAS DE DEUX

He waltzed up to the table, not afraid to take a chance
He said, sir, would you mind it if I asked your girl to dance
I said, good sir, it's up to her, she makes up her own mind
I think that you could see he was the Casanova kind

You graciously consented 'cause you knew I wouldn't care
He thought he was the model of a modern Fred Astaire
I don't believe I've ever seen a better pas de deux
He must have tried a hundred styles
      before the band was through

      He held you tight, he wanted to impress you
      His eager eyes tried vainly to undress you
      I could tell that he was longing to caress you
      When you held him off I whispered darlin' bless you

He threw you in the air and then he stepped upon your gown
I didn't know who'd be the first to let the other down
He didn't watch his step so he was in for quite a fall
But all-in-all, I'd say you were the best bell of the ball

I'II bet he was dismayed, at least his face turned kinda red
To think that you'd reject him and return to me instead
You must have knocked him over when you very firmly said
I think I'll have the last fling on my hubby's waterbed

Night, Night

THE SEA, THE SKY, AND WHO AM I

Alone, I sit on the sandy beach
And watch the waves caress the shore
I see the liquid fingers reach
For loamy secrets to explore

I feel the grains sift through my hand
A few remain and cling
As though their stay were somehow planned
A lasting sort of thing

How many are the grains of sand
Spawned by the mighty sea
How difficult to understand
What causes this to be

The ocean is a galaxy
Sands like the stars abound
How infinite the mystery
My soul the sands surround

If Providence created this
And all were meant to be
Would it not be quite remiss
If a tiny part weren't me

I JUST NEED TO BE THANKFUL MORE

Sometimes I get down on my knees
And start off oh Lord will you please
Forgetting all the good that came before
Lord, I don't need more to be thankful for
I just need to be thankful more

Sometimes I think He isn't near
And that He really doesn't hear
Forgetting all the things he had in store
Lord, I don't need more to be thankful for
I just need to be thankful more

Sometimes I knock and don't receive
And I'm not sure that I believe
Forgetting that He opened up the door
Lord, I don't need more to be thankful for
I just need to be thankful more

      I do believe one time he said you're welcome
      Trust me 'cause I know what's best for you
      If you don't get all you're prayin' for
      It's because I'm up here with a better view

                          . . .

So now I stop and look around
And count the blessings that abound
Rememb'rin' that I am no longer poor
Lord, I don't need more to be thankful for
I just need to be thankful more

I CAN'T HELP WONDERIN' WHY A WONDERFUL WOMAN LOVES ME

I can't help wondrin' why a wonderful woman loves me
She is everything that a wonderful woman should be
She's my lover—She's my life
She's a mother—She's my wife
And when we're one, she loves me so wonderfully

I can't help wondrin' why a wonderful woman loves me
She could have had any man she wanted so easily
She is pretty, She's a doll
She is witty, She's my all
And when we're done, she still holds me passionately

      I'm not very handsome, I'm not very smart
      I'm not very clever, she knew from the start
      I'm not very funny, I'm no work of art
      But I know her lovin' comes straight from her heart

I can't help wondrin' why a wonderful woman loves me
She's so warm and so wanted and so womanly
She's so teasin', she's so sweet
She's so pleasin', she's so neat
I'm just a man—but forever a one-woman man I will be

END OF A BAT AFFAIR

When I was just a little ghoul, my mummy said to me
You're growing up so very fast—it's been a century
When you mature you must endure a lot of misery
But stay away from vampire bats—o-positive-uh-Iy

Believe me dear a vampire isn't looking for a pet
You'll wake up every hundred years and find your neck is wet
He'll woo you and subdue you—he can't wait to stick it to you
Right off the bat, you'll find that you will need a tourniquet

Don't ever date a vampire, never have a sad affair
A bat flies off the handle with his nose up in the air
Even when the stakes are high—he will leave you high and dry
He often leaves his coffin just to get into your hair

A werewolf only combs his face and wants a bite goodnight
It's only when the moon is full he really sees the light
Once a month I must confess—werewolves suffer some distress
Your hair will surely stand on end if you can stand the sight

A werewolf isn't all that bad, but bats don't even floss
And if you dare to meet a pair, you'll need a double cross
Realize that as he hangs—he don't sterilize his fangs
So if you just must have a bird, go find an albatross

So listen to me little ghoul, and heed my sage advice
A werewolf's warm and fuzzy, but a vampire isn't nice
If you believe that you're a vamp—you better think it twice
You'll be better off if you don't hang out with the mice

FORTY-FIVE YEARS

For forty-five years she's made my coffee
Forty-five years she's made my tea
Forty-five years she's made my bed so wrinkle-free
But best of all
My little doll
Has made great love to me

For forty-five years she's been my partner
Forty-five years she's been my pal
Forty-five years she's been my one and only gal
      But best of all
      My little doll
      Made children oh so well

      Her hair was black and now it's salt and pepper gray
      And when she smiles a little crease appears
      Still I swear I wouldn't have her any other way
      My love of her and need for her
                has grown throughout the years

For forty-five years she's been my darlin'
Forty-five years my dearest friend
Forty-five years on her I always could depend
      But best of all
      My little doll
      Never let it end

PRINCIPIA PRINCESS

She was homecoming queen, she was queen of everything
She was dutiful and beautiful and stately
She was fair and debonair and had a very special flair
She had all the royal grace that comes innately

Principia Princess—Tiara in her hair
If she ever lets her hair down, I wanna be there

I was not of royalty but she had all my loyalty
I was clumsy and afraid to ever date her
I could never take rejection from a girl of such perfection
I was sure she'd never date a second-rater

I was a clown without a crown and I knew I'd get turned down
But decided what the hell give it a try
When I asked her for a date, she said darlin' don't be late
I've been waiting for so long I thought I'd die

She said they all made me a queen but I'm as lonesome as can be
God has graced me that is true but I'm so lonely
I'm so grateful I can serve, but I'm so glad you had the nerve
To ask me out so now you are my one and only

· · ·

She said I sure don't need champagne, a quarter-pounder will do
A simple walk and friendly talk are what I've missed
I like funny picture shows, popcorn, and a beer or two
I just love it when I'm hugged and warmly kissed

Well, the night-ful was delightful and we really had a ball
And I don't believe I've had such lovin" since
She really let her tresses fall and man the greatest joy of all
Was that night I became her Student Prince!

Principia Princess—Tiara in her hair
When she finally let her hair down, THANK GOD I WAS
    THERE!

SEMPER FIT

I've

nev-

er

seen a

fat

Ma-

rine and

I

re-

fer to

him OR her

JENNY WREN

Jenny Wren, you've flown away again
Have you found yourself a feathered friend
Why do you desert me
Why you wanna hurt me
I know you'll be back but don't know when

Jenny Wren, you've flown away again
Have you found yourself another wren
Why do you forsake me
Why you wanna break me
I don't wanna know where you have been

> Every time you've had your little fling
> You come back to me with broken wing
> You say it's my love that makes it mend
> Then you go and fly away again

Jenny Wren, you've flown away again
You will break your wing again and then
You'll come home to rest
And find an empty nest
I have flown away like Jenny Wren

HAPA HAOLE

I can't exactly figure out
Just what I'm s'posed to be
I'll tell you what it's all about
The maybe you'll tell me

My Daddy's in the Air Force
My Mama's from Japan
I was born in Tennessee—source
Of where it all began

I'm a little Oriental
And there's rebel in my kin
And the problem gets quite mental
When you add the Irish in

I could be called Eurasian
But some might get annoyed
I'm not a pure Caucasian
Cause my Mama's Mongoloid

If I put the two together
Then Caucaloid I'd be
But then I don't know whether
Mongocasian best suits me

. . .

I'm growing up in Germany
Which adds to the confusion
But let us stop and see if we
Canfind a good solution

Perhaps you might agree with me
Stop searching while we can
I have a nationality
I'm a real American!

IF YOU'LL COME INTO MY ARMS

Let me put my arms around you dear 'cause
I have been there too
I know that awful feelin' when the world is down on you
I can feel your hesitation
Know your hopeless isolation
if you'll come into my arms we'll see it through

Let me put my arms around you dear and help to ease the pain
I know that awful feelin' when your cryin's all in vain
If you'll only let me near you
Let me listen, let me hear you
If you'll come into my arms I can explain

     Wanna know how I know how you feel
     Why I know you feelin's really very real
     Don't you know that I have loved you through the years
     That is how I know what brings about the tears

Let me put my arms around you dear and
     then you'll surely know
We've known that awful feelin' but at last it's gonna go
When you know I am your true one
You'll no longer be the blue one
If you'll come into my arms we'll make it so

LOOK BESIDE YOU

When you're feelin' down and out, there's no need to look about
Look beside you, I am with you all the way
When you feel like it's the end, when you really need a friend
Look beside you, dear, and know I'm here to stay

When you wanna scream and shout, or just wanna sit and pout
Look beside you, I am with you all the way
When you're feelin' really bad, when you think
    that you've been had
Look beside you, dear, and know I'm here to stay

    When you're really feelin' down
    When you wanna fret and frown
    Come along and smile a while
    Cryin's really not your style

When you really need a friend, one on whom you can depend
Look beside you, I am with you all the way
There's no need for you to doubt, that's what love is all about
Look beside you, dear, and know I'm here to stay

SOMETHIN' BLUE

Somethin' old
'N somethin' blue
But I'm not standin' next to you
Darlin' when you say I do
I will become the somethin' blue

My love was old
While yours was new
I can't believe we're really through
You had a different point of view
Now I've become the somethin' blue

      I'll never know what I did wrong
      Why you were stringin' me along
      I didn't know
      I couldn't see
      That you were truly foolin' me

I never had a single clue
I guess my loss was overdue
I was borrowed
And you knew
That I'd become the somethin' blue

GOT M'BUTTS 'N M'BEER

Saw an item in the news
Rich old boy was born to lose
Lost a bundle in a scam
Now he's dead and here I am

      I am just a plain old guy
      Fame and fortune passed me by
      So my needs are very few
      You 'n a brew n' a butt or two

            Never drove a fancy car
            Never traveled very far
            Never tasted caviar

              Got m'butts 'n m'beer
              N' you m'dear
              That's all I'll ever need

He committed suicide
Shot himself and then he died
Kept his feelin's all inside
I ain't got that kind of pride

    I am just a simple man
    Never been a fancy dan
    Make my livin' best I can
    I ain't got a fav'rite bran

        Never saw a shootin' star
        All I own's my old guitar
        Keep my savings in a jar

            Got m'butts 'n m'beer
            N' you m'dear
            That's all I'll ever need
            That's all I'll ever need

MY BUDDY JOHN HILL

My buddy John was quite a guy
He loved to drive and he loved to fly
He'd disappear at the slightest whim
But he was always there when I needed him

My buddy John had quite a line
He knew the ropes and he knew his wine
Women and song and the best of taste
And he said the rest was just a waste

My buddy John was an engineer
He made those goonies git in gear
He kept 'em flyin' true and straight
And comin' home we were never late

My buddy John was an NCO
There was very little he didn't know
But way down deep he was G.l. Joe
And everybody loved him so

My buddy John has flown away
I know we'll meet again some day
He's up there somewhere in the sky
Teachin' angels how to fly

My buddy John was many things
But now he's wearin' different wings
I've heard the wine is heavenly
So slow down John, save one for me

His Radioman,
Murph

COUNSELING AND GUIDANCE

Dear parents of poor Normal, we have lately done the Kuder
Results are still informal as received from the computer
But in the case of your child, I believe that we should hurry
For when the test scores were compiled,
      it was cause enough to worry
It looks as though this child has no preferences at all
And though it seems quite mild, it's a fate we could forestall
To have no interests in ten can hardly be deferred
It seems to me most proper then, that his case be referred
Of course, with your approval, our good principal's assistance
May prevent the child's removal or at least end his resistance
Advise if you agree with this, please let me know today
We can't afford to be remiss, Miss Unaware, B.A.

Dear teacher of our poor lad, we frankly are amazed
To think our lad could do so bad has simply got us dazed
We don't know Kuder from MacGruder but do
      what you must do
We can't afford a tutor, so we guess it's up to you
We trust that you can teach him, with experience and skill
Or the principal can reach him, and with interest instill
We trust that you will treat him with dignified finesse
We want him a complete him, nothing more and nothing less
We suppose if interests he achieves, you'll score a big success
Sincerely, The Naives; M.R. and M.R.S.

Miss Unaware, attention please, in reference to this case
Discipline cannot appease nor preference replace
It's not an admin job you see to analyze Form E
The guidance staff quite readily can advise of the necessity
To take the action that's required to help the boy decide
That an education is desired if he wants a job outside
Maintaining peace among the staff and pleasing our good mayor
Keeping costs down on the graph and appeasing each taxpayer
Principals have quite a chore, I'm sure you will agree
I simply cannot handle more to any great degree
I'm referring present case at hand to our guidance staff today
Sincerely, Mr. Understand, A.B., B.S., MA.

Miss Unaware, I have your case, it's been referred to me
The problem is most commonplace, I'm sure you will agree
I'm not aware of anything that can't be surely solved
With patience any little thing can slowly be resolved
Now in the case of this poor lad, there's no problem in achieving
It's just a temporary fad, say, a question of believing
His interests have gone astray, a fact we can't ignore
He only needs to find his way, that's what counselors are for
The problem seems emotional, but let's not take a chance
The Doctor's so devotional, he can tell in one quick glance
If medication is required, we'll solicit his advice
His dedication is inspired, and opinions so concise
The clinic's near so I'll refer the case to them today

. . .

For us, they're able to assure that he's physically o.k
I'll let you know what we've decided, what we can assess
Sincerely, Miss Guided, B.S., M.A., and M.S.

Miss Unaware, I'm writing to provide you my advice
There has been some oversighting when
        we really should look twice
Medication's not a cure-all for a problem of this kind
It's not a health referral for it's only in his mind
A character disorder is evidenced by facts
A neurosis of some order can be seen by how he acts
Folks think kids are bubonic when it's just a little whim
Problems that aren't chronic have a way of looking grim
Since this case appears more mental than medical in kind
I would be detrimental if I left his psyche behind
The school psychologist should see the problem child today
It's simply not a case for me, I'll refer it right away
He may find a psychosis when he gets the facts from me
Sincerely, Diagnosis, B.A., B.S., and M.D.

Miss Unaware, I have the notes connected with this case
And all the other anecdotes are falling into place
As school psychologist I say you should not be upset
I diagnosed the case today and I'm not troubled yet
This student isn't very slow, although he's not so fast
He never seems the first to go, but never ends up last
The type of therapy to use is difficult to say
I wouldn't want you to confuse the cure in any way

A pleasant personality, achievement with the best
The only problem seems to be that he's lost his interest
A classic paradox appears to enter on the scene
But he succeeds who perseveres with problems not routine
The Kuder simply indicates no interest appears
But consider all the other traits and the problem disappears
If you still wonder what to do, perhaps it would be nice
To contact Normal's parents who may offer some advice
I trust that the resultant facts will provide the final key
Sincerely, A. Consultant, B.S., M.S., Ph.D.

Miss Unaware, remember us, we're Normal's Mom and Dad
Seems we created quite a fuss, because of our poor lad
It appears he had no aptitude based on a Kuder score
Well, since we've watched his attitude in hopes of learning more
A fact has been uncovered, and we find to our dismay
We have recently discovered he was home with us that day
He didn't take the test at all, and we further must purvey
He graduates from "U" this fall and is now a PBK
Those machines give no reprieves, we're afraid we must confess
Sincerely, The Naives, M.R. and M.R.S

ACT ONE
SCENE ONE

(The scene is the Belaire High School Teen Canteen and the year is 1967. Belaire is an affluent residential small city in the Midwest whose citizens consist primarily of physicians, attorneys, and high-ranking executives of the business world. The Belaire High School graduating seniors are meeting in the Teen Canteen to celebrate the homecoming of their State champion football team. When the curtain opens, some seniors are already in the Canteen, notably the champion chess team and champion debate team.

The Canteen is equipped with the usual one-on-one games such as table tennis, hockey and chess. A colorful juke box sits against the back wall. There is a small concession stand in a far corner. The center of the Canteen has room for dancing. On the walls are signs that read "Class of '67", "Senior Night", and "Seniors Only."

The young people of Belaire always dress to perfection—coat and tie and expensive party dresses. They favor their school colors of red and white. In their own minds, they are the ultimate sophisticates—in truth, they are arrogant young snobs.

Except Lenny Lee and Jenny Wren, the two senior class misfits and outcasts of Belaire society. These two dress in blue jeans, white short-sleeved shirts and wear little white aprons. It is their misfortune to be unskilled and poor, and it is their duty to run the concession stand in the Canteen to serve their fellow classmates.

As the story begins, a few seniors—those who are most scholastically oriented – are waiting for the football team and accompanying cheerleaders to arrive. The team has just won the state championship and can hardly wait to boast of their conquest.)(The football team and cheerleaders enter boisterously.)

THE MIGHTY TEAM

TEAM:

We're the mightiest of men and best of teams by far

And so we won again, the world knows who we are

On a scale of one to ten, we're twenty over par

But then, we've always been a super star

CHEERLEADERS

You're our heroes, we adore you

We would do almost anything for you

We admire you, we desire you

And when you're tired and expired—we'll restore you

TEAM:

People say we're made of stone, and others say of rocks

Admire our muscle tone; we love to clean their clocks

We've been known to knock them off their bloody blocks

We're on a golden throne, we're super jocks

CHEERLEADERS:

You're our heroes, and we love you

We would put no one above you

Don't abuse us, or misuse us

And don't bruise us—is all we ask of you

TEAM:

There's no doubt we're number one, there is no doubt at all
The fans all shout that we're top gun, and walking tall
All about us there are none who can recall
A team that's ever been more on the ball

CHEERLEADERS:

You're our heroes, we're behind you
You're one of a kind, we remind you
Wine and dine us, intertwine us
And when you're down and unwound, we'll rewind you
You're our heroes, we're devoted
Your achievements have been duly noted
If you want us
Don't confront us
All your words better be sugar-coated

(Following a great deal of dialogue, in the Teen Canteen, the wealthy kids brag about their possessions)

THE AFFLUENT SOCIETY

BOYS:

We excel at our billiard tables

GIRLS:

We look swell in our silver sables

ALL:

There's very little that we haven't got

BOYS:

We've got leather in all our cars

GIRLS:

Our Mothers all are D.A.R.s

ALL:

There's sleeping room for fourteen on our yacht

BOYS:

Our spas and tennis courts have lights

GIRLS:

Our villa's on the highest heights

ALL:

Our cooks and maids have bachelor's degrees

BOYS:

We all have heated swimming pools

GIRLS:

And marble in the vestibules

ALL:

You bet our cats are blue-point Siamese

BOYS:

Our polo pony's pedigreed

GIRLS:

Our greyhounds are a special breed

ALL:

We sit on silk and sleep on satin sheets

BOYS:

We have a naughty hide-a-way

GIRLS:

We have a haughty Swiss chalet

ALL:

We only stay in Hilton's private suites

BOYS:

So now it's time to pick a school

GIRLS:

And always mind the golden rule

ALL:

The rulers are the ones who've got the gold

TEDDY:

The Ivy League's the only place

The only place to show your face

A League degree is the only one to hold

(Lenny and Jenny, the class misfits sing of their "affluent society")

LENNY AND JENNY'S AFFLUENT SOCIETY

LENNY:

I've got a little two-room flat

JENNY:

I've got a yellow alley cat

BOTH:

The water in the tub is never hot

LENNY:

I'll never own a classy car

JENNY:

I keep my savings in a jar

BOTH:

We DO have cotton sheets upon the cot

LENNY:

My table is the fold-up kind

JENNY:

I can't remember when I've "dined"

BOTH:

We just don't have a thing that's very fit

LENNY:

I've got a bike for my paper route

JENNY:

No girl will ever take you out

BOTH:

'Cause who wants handle-bars on which to sit

LENNY:

I just don't have the brains they do

JENNY:

Can you imagine my "debut"

BOTH:

Let's face it dear we don't have any class

LENNY:

I'll never get a scholarship

JENNY:

I'll never own a satin slip

BOTH:

We'll always be the bronze and not the brass

LENNY:

I regret I spoiled their goal

JENNY:

I'm sorry I can't play the role

BOTH:

It seems that we were born to swim up-stream

LENNY:

I'm not the athletic kind

JENNY:

I'm sorta the pathetic kind

BOTH:

We've NEVER been a MEMBER of the TEAM'

(Lenny has deserted Jenny in the Canteen. Jenny sings of her unrequited love)

THE HARDER I TRY

JENNY:

The harder I try, the more he neglects me

The harder I try, the less he respects me

He always seems so far away

He can't know how much I despair

And try hard as I may

He just seems unaware

The harder I try, the more that he grieves me

The harder I try, the less he believes me

I've tried so hard to let him know

It's nearly more than I can bear

What on earth can I do to show

Him how much I care

Maybe he'll come around some day

Maybe I'll find another way

Maybe he is right and I'm all wrong

Maybe I've been coming on too strong

The harder I try, the more he discards me

The harder I try, the less he regards me

I only want to touch his hand

If he would give me one small chance

How can I make him understand

How much I need romance

END OF ACT ONE
Scene One

ACT ONE
SCENE TWO

(Lenny is in Marine Corps basic training. The squad has just returned from a grueling hike. Lenny wants to quit but his teammates won't let him)

I'LL NEVER BECOME A MEMBER OF THE CORPS

LENNY:

I can't make it, I can't take it anymore

I'm so sore I cannot get up off the floor

I don't have any pride

I'm hurtin' so inside

I don't know why I tried

I'll never become a member of the corps

SQUAD:

You're a member of the team, like it or not

You gotta get on the beam, have you forgot

You took an oath to serve

Now you can't lose your nerve

And most likely if you scream, we'll ALL get shot

LENNY:

On a scale of one to ten, I'm minus four

I was born so awful ugly, dumb and poor

I'm hurtin' from the shame

I've only me to blame

I'll never become a member of the corps

SQUAD:

You're a member of the team, not second rate

Develop some self-esteem, co-op-er-ate

We all are gonna make it

Show us you can take it

Get up a head of steam and pull your weight

LENNY:

In my life this was my only chance to score

But I never really knew what was in store

I guess I'm not so strong

I never will belong

I'll never become a member of the corps

SQUAD:

You're a member of the team, don't alibi

You're not living in a dream, it's do or die

We know it takes a lot

But give it all you got

You can make the team supreme if you'll just TRY, TRY, TRY

You can make the team supreme if you'll just TRY

(Sergeant Leathery overhears his squad complaining and gives them a sermon)

DO ME PROUD

SERGEANT LEATHERY:

Poor babies—poor wimps—do you need a pacifier

No maybes—you shrimps—I can set your ass afire

Nobody EVER quits on me—YOU HEAR?

So let me tell you very loud and clear

Get offa your butts and on your feet

Get outta the shade and in the heat

Poor dummies—poor dinks—don't EVER make me a liar

Poor scummies—poor finks—I just can't stand a CRIER

You listen—you dunce—I'm tellin' you clear and loud

Stop pissin'—just once—you're gonna do me proud

It takes all you got to be a part

You gotta have guts and a lot of heart

Get offa your case and into pride

Get outta this place and into stride

Don't slow up—GET MEAN—you can make it if you care

Just grow up—MARINE—and you can make it ANYWHERE

(The squad is determined to make Sgt Leathery proud of them in this reprise)

DO YOU PROUD

SQUAD:

Denote how—we show—standin' tall and hand salutin'
We know how—to go—that's not all, we're good at shootin'
Nobody EVER quits on you—NO WAY
So let us tell you what we gotta say
We go by the book—it's always right
We know how to look—and how to fight
Don't worry 'bout us—we've had the best kind of trainin'
Don't ever doubt us—you'll never hear us complainin'

We're upright and straight—our heads are never bowed
We're uptight and great—we're gonna do you proud
We got what it takes and maybe more
We'll do you so proud of us in the corps
You trained us real good—so we are wise
Look out for the dolls—we're normal guys
We know that—we're hot—still no matter how she tries
We know what—and not—and we will NEVER FRAT-ER-NIZE

(The squad has put one over on Sgt Leathery by helping Lenny police up the barracks. Now they have all escaped to the U. S. O. in town as the Sergeant inspects the area)

I GOTTA HIDE MY PRIDE INSIDE

SERGEANT LEATHERY:

They're so young and they're so green
But they're 'bout the best I've seen
I gotta make 'em lean and mean
I gotta make a good Marine
I gotta know that patience pays
I only got a few more days
I can't afford no more delays
To make 'em change a thousand ways
I cannot show—they must not know
Each one of them is like a son
I gotta hide my pride inside
The pride for every single one
I only had a little while
A little while to change their style
They better never see me smile
I gotta love 'em—rank and file

END OF ACT ONE
Scene Two

ACT ONE
SCENE THREE

(Miss Matilda is the tough-but-oh-so-gentle supervisor of the U.S.O. She believes it is her duty to warn all of her young hostesses about fraternization with GIs.)

BE CAREFUL OF A MODERN MINUTEMAN

SAILOR: *(Pleading)*

But, Miss Matilda, a sailor is trustworthy and loyal!

MISS MATILDA:

What?
Be careful of a sailor in from sea
He takes liberties when he's on liberty
You will hear him sing the Navy blues
But, dear, you are the one who'll lose
You'll find out when the tide's out—so is he
He loves his ship and calls his ship a she
He takes a dip and he's an absentee
You can't compete with a neat affair
Or with his fleet afloat out there
At break of day, he's sailing out to sea

U.S.O. GIRLS:

When the boys begin to flirt,
We all go on red alert

We tell 'em—give up—you can't win
We don't give out and we don't give in

SOLDIER: *(Pleading)*

But, Miss Matilda, a soldier is helpful and friendly!

MISS MATILDA:

What?
Be careful of a soldier so I say
There's none so tricky as a green beret
He is fit, it's true, and he's all male
He loves to hit that dusty trail
    He's over hill and dale at break of day
He never calls his M-16 a gun
He says his gun is only meant for fun
If you don't quite know just what that means
You better button up your jeans
He'll "be all that he can be"—then he'll run

U.S.O. GIRLS:

When the boys begin to flirt
We all go on red alert
We tell 'em—give up—you can't win
We don't give out and we don't give in

AIRMAN: (Pleading)

But, Miss Matilda, an airman is courteous and kind!

MISS MATILDA:

What?
Be careful of an airman so I say
He makes a strike and then he goes astray
He's so fast that you'll regret
You've met a super-sonic jet
When the bombing's over, he just flies away
An airman thinks that he's in outer space
He tries to space you out when you embrace
He looks upon you as a learner
You are just his after-burner
He will leave your base, oh yes, without a trace

U.S.O. GIRLS:

When the boys begin to flirt
We all go on red alert
We tell 'em—give up—you can't win
We don't give out and we don't give in

COAST GUARD: *(Pleading)*

But, Miss Matilda, a coastguardsman is obedient, cheerful and
thrifty.

MISS MATILDA:

Be careful of the Coast Guard so I say
He waits 'til the coast is clear to have his way
He pretends he's on a rescue
And in no time he's undressed you
Then he'll cut out on his cutter 'cross the bay

His tenders all get tender loving care
But to share his tenderness is very rare
A life line is his way to save
But a bride to him is a tidal wave
Take care the line he feeds you's not a snare

U.S.O. GIRLS:

When the boys begin to flirt
We all go on red alert
We tell 'em—give up—you can't win
We don't give out and we don't give in

MARINE: *(Pleading)*

But, Miss Matilda, a marine is brave, clean and reverent.

MISS MATILDA:

What?
Be careful of a member of the corps
A few GOOD girls he isn't looking for
He loves his combat hand-to-hand
And loves to wrestle in the sand
He brings along a buddy to keep score
He field strips anyone in nothing flat
He does a thousand push-ups on a mat
But if you are ever under there
So in the dark and unaware
You'll soon wake up and wonder where he's at

MISS MATILDA & GIRLS:

BE CAREFUL OF A MODERN MINUTEMAN!

(The female service personnel slightly resent the fact that the men are getting all the attention and are determined that THEIR case be heard)

A MODERN MINUTEWOMAN

ALL THE SERVICE:

A woman who strives to be like a man lacks ambition

WOMEN:

So let us tell you WE ARE IN COMMAND

We've got something you don't have—it's intuition

And ambition like you'd never understand

There's no machine that has been built that we can't handle

Modern woman knows what it is all about

Pound for pound, you guys can't even hold a candle

When you're in doubt—just shout—we'll bail you out

We would never ask you out so don't get nervous

We can pull our weight and earn our bread

SOLO: *(Spoken sarcastically)*

We prefer an acting assistant executive to the

Deputy Undersecretary of Defense in CIVIL SERVICE

ALL:

Where they don't neglect but give respect instead

(The servicemen feel sorry for themselves. They swear they wouldn't hurt a flea—or girl)

WE'RE INNOCENT AS WE CAN BE

ALL OF THE:

We're innocent as we can be and totally discrete

SERVICEMEN:

We never lie or ever try to sweep her off her feet

The kiss we give is just a peck

We never nibble on her neck

A harmless hug around her waist will keep her chaste and sweet

We're innocent as we can be and totally discrete

We never lie or ever try to sweep her off her feet

The kiss we give is just a peck

We never nibble on her neck

A harmless hug around her waist will keep her chaste and sweet

We're innocent as we can be and totally benign

We're really shy and always try to walk a narrow line

We never threaten or demand

We only want to hold her hand

We positively think it's fine to say she's just a friend of mine

We treat her like we would our little sister

Sometimes it takes a big man to resist her

Don't ever fret or sweat or ever hold your breath

Because to be a Daddy SCARES US HALF TO DEATH

We're innocent as we can be and totally aware

. . .

We never lust, just trust that we give tender loving care

Please help us get up off our knees

'Cause all we want's a little squeeze

So don't beware, we're much too square to have a daring love affair

(Lenny lags behind his team and kindly Miss Matilda senses his loneliness. It's the girl he left behind.)

THE PERFECT GIFT

MISS MATILDA:

I'll tell you what I think the perfect gift would be

It doesn't cost a thing—it's absolutely free

It comes from some great power that we know little of

That wondrous feeling that we feel when first we love

I'll tell you what's so precious—it's when first you know

That the warmth you feel inside you will continue to grow

You sense it in your heart—you know it in your soul

It's the only thing that makes someone completely whole

So take your little gift and always hold it dear

Cherish it and always keep it near

The gift of love must be secure—so sweet and pure

If you keep it safe, you know it always will endure

END OF ACT ONE
Scene Three

(NOTE: ACT ONE, Scene Four, takes place at the Naval Nurses' Training School. It is all dialogue between Jenny and her best friend, Lisa. Lisa is a feisty little character who will follow Jenny into the Navy and subsequently into combat.)

ACT ONE
SCENE FIVE

(At a lonely outpost in Vietnam, Lenny prays that Jenny will not enter the Navy nor look for him.)

LENNY'S LAMENT

LENNY:

Dear God

Deliver me from this confusion

And Jenny from her terrible delusion

If you could tell her—somehow—just to wait for me

I'd get down on my knees

And thank you—so gratefully

You see—Jenny's never had a family—except me and her cat

But Lord, you know she deserves much more than that

She deserves silk dresses, sir, and satin sheets

And tasty treats—and lots of sweets

But we don't have things like that where I'm at

Who has dominion over me—authority—supremacy

There is no empathy—probably—never will be

They tell me what to do, that's a fact

They even tell me who to love and how to act

How can that be—who knows my mind and heart better

The corps is my family—the only one I've ever had

I'm a member of the team and that's where I belong

But—
I'm perplexed—and so confused
And so in love with her
Why does that have to be bad
I don't know but I gotta be strong
And somehow—somehow—see it through
But—
What to do
I can't have my cake and eat it too
It seems to me the choice is painfully clear
I'm not allowed to have two loves—or so I fear
I gotta choose just one—my love or my career
God!
I just don't know
I JUST DON'T KNOW

END OF ACT ONE

ACT TWO
SCENE ONE

(Lisa is in the intensive care unit of the field hospital in the middle of the night. She sits at an old desk and writes to her Mom)

LISA'S LETTER

LISA:

Dear Mom,

All the time I was a kid, I always did just what you bid

When I was just a little tad, you said, my dear, it's time we had

a nurse in the family

You told me candidly, you said

In all the universe

There's none so noble as a nurse

To serve mankind is a GLORIOUS profession—so you said

Now you deserve this NOTORIOUS confession—'fore I'm dead

I always knew someday I'd be a nanny in a nursery

The pinks and blues and pastel hues seemed neat and sweet to me

Well what I got is olive drab and mummies lying on a slab

You never said that I might dread this man-made misery

My "kiddies" all are six feet tall and weigh a couple hundred pounds

And when I make my midnight rounds, it's clear they've had their ups and downs

Instead of baby sighs I hear obscenities so loud and clear

You never said that I might dread the odors and the sounds

My tresses are an awful mess—You call these friggin' things a dress

My boots were meant for horse manure—oh, man, I need a mani-
cure

The only I.V.s in my mind—were the growing up a brick wall
kind

I never thought I'd give a shot on a very hairy bare behind

For men to mend we gotta sew up

That is when I tend to throw up

You never said that I might dread the smell of iodine

But still—You know what, Mom—

Teachers have hours of homework to do

Young secretaries get dictated to

Park rangerettes do get lost in the woods

Salesladies get sold a big bill of goods

Models get manhandled 'til they say ouch

Actresses often get cast on a couch

Housewives get homier day after day

Chorus girls spend all their pay on Ben-gay

So MANY professions I can think of

What's better than this?

NONE OF THE ABOVE

You never said that life for me would be a bed of roses

A young girl grows and knows she'll do whatever Mom proposes

I look around

And have to smile

I guess I'll stick around awhile

. . .

What would they do without us, Mom?
With THAT—this letter closes
Your loving daughter
Lisa

(Bruno, a very proud Marine captain has been wounded in his eyes and cannot see. He wakes up in the middle of the night and calls for Lisa. In life, he believes there is more than the eye can see.)

SOME PEOPLE HAVE EYES

BRUNO:

Some people have eyes, but they don't realize
That they still cannot see
Some people have eyes, but they can't visualize
The true reality
Seeing is believing is a very, very narrow point
Open up their mind—and they"ll find—that that their
    heart sees things too
Some people have eyes, but they still criticize
Everything that they see
Some people have eyes, but they're not very w
They try hard not to be
They must have a look at every pretty little bro
To prove it is there
Look up at the sun and wonder
If the weather will be truly fair
NOT ME!

The soft touch of a gentle April shower
The fragrance of a woman or a flower
The coolness of a breeze upon my face
The solitude of a very quiet place
The laughter of the children when at play
The warbling of a wren at break of day
These miracles of life are but a start

To see the things that lie within my heart
Some people have eyes, but they still compromise
All the beauty they see
Some people have eyes, but they still advertise
Only life's misery
Why that attitude—where is the gratitude
For being so alive
I've got so much to live for
God knows I'm going to GIVE IT A TRY

(Lisa has been hurt in love before, but she is falling for Bruno. She warns them both to be careful)

HANDLE WITH CARE

LISA:

Some lovers wear their heart on their sleeve

Some lovers are so young and naïve

So I must beg you darlin' to be fair

My heart has a label—it says fragile

Handle with care

Some lovers just refuse to believe

Some lovers think it's fun to deceive

So I must beg you darlin' to beware

My heart has a label—it says fragile

Handle with care

My heart is soft as a sigh

So handle it delicately

You don't even have to try

It breaks—so easily

Some lovers don't know what they'll receive

Some lovers don't know how they'll bereave

So I must beg you darlin' hear my prayer

My heart has a label—it says fragile

Handle with care

(A very concerned General Resolute visits the hospital in the middle of the night. Lisa is terrified but the General puts her at ease. He shows his love for his troops in his prayer for their recovery)

GIVE THEM TOMORROW

GENERAL RESOLUTE:

Our Father

These are your sons

They are the best that you created—they're the gallant ones

As You loved Your Son—then you must know my sorrow

Their lives had just begun

Dear Father —Give them tomorrow

Our Father —Please hear my plea

This is the Earth that you created—help us keep it free

No doubt we know how—but there's no time to borrow

You must not take them now

Dear Father

Give them tomorrow

Thine is the kingdom and the glory and the power

Do not forsake them; help them make it through this hour

They are Your children, Sir, and when their blood is shed

It is by Your grace that every trace is the same shade of red

Our Father

These are my men

Thy kingdom come—thy will be done

Please make them well again

They're too young to have sinned very much

But they all know great sorrow

Their lives had just begun

Dear Father

Give them tomorrow

And another tomorrow—tomorrow

(Jenny has relieved Lisa who has gone home. Jenny lovingly considers her nursing career to be a very noble profession with a definite purpose)

THE PURPOSE OF A NURSE

JENNY:

The purpose of a nurse is to care for you
To be aware, and give all she can give
The purpose of a nurse is to share with you
To share with you a prayer for you to live
The purpose of a nurse is to be with you
To be with you and help you to endure
The purpose of a nurse is to see you through
To see you through, to comfort, to cure
Sometimes I'm afraid that the fight for life might be in vain
And all I can do is try to help you ease the pain
Somewhere, perhaps, there's a far better purpose for you
Sometimes I'm afraid that your purpose on
  Earth might be through
Then suddenly, a miracle happens and we don't know why
With eyes wide open you decide to give life one more try
You've taken the turn we've been hoping and praying for
And then do I know the wonderful purpose of a nurse once more

(Jenny discovers that Lenny is the critically wounded G.I. recently brought into the hospital)

YOU'LL NEVER LEAVE ME NOW

JENNY:

Is this the miracle for which I've prayed

LENNY:

It seems I've been asleep for a long time

JENNY:

Oh, Lord, forgive me, I was so afraid

LENNY:

It seems I've had a very long long hill to climb

JENNY:

This, I vow, you'll never leave me now

LENNY:

Oh, Jen, I think I've know it all along

JENNY:

This, I vow, I'll pull you through somehow

LENNY:

That it was you who kept me safe and strong—safe and strong

JENNY:

I'll never let you slip away from me

LENNY:

You're with me now and that's where you belong

JENNY:

As God is merciful, I guarantee

BOTH:

Now you're here and nothing can go wrong

END OF ACT TWO
Scene One

ACT TWO
SCENE THREE

(Lenny reflects that if he only knew then what he knows now, everything would be much better. Jenny is skeptical and tells Lenny he is kidding himself)

IF I COULD GO BACK AGAIN

LENNY:

    If I only knew then, all the things I know now

    If I could go back again, I'd make it better somehow

    I'd make many amends, and have so many friends

    I'd stand out in the crowd

JENNY:

    STOP IT! Stop feeling sorry for yourself.

    If you could go back again, it wouldn't change things one bit

    You couldn't say what you meant, you'd be a big hypocrite

    You could play golf and lose, lick your boss's new shoes

    Oh yes, you'd be a hit

LENNY:

    If I only knew then, what I now realize

    If I could go back again, what a pleasant surprise

    If I had one more turn, I'd have less to unlearn

    Now I've opened my eyes

JENNY:

If you could go back again, you'd have to swallow your pride
You could really fit in, just keep your feelings inside
You could cheat on your tax, and scratch all of their backs
Oh yes, you'd turn the tide

LENNY:

If I only knew then, now that I see the light
If I could go back again, I'd make everything right
If I had one more chance, I'd take a new stance
I'd no longer take flight

JENNY:

If you could go back again, you think they'd open the door
If you were like all of them, you'd one helluva bore
You could look down your nose, and borrow tailor-made clothes
But you'd always be poor

LENNY:

Only now do I know that the world doesn't owe me a living
Only now can I show that I know how to go on forgiving
I'm no longer afraid to be loved and to love in return
Now I'm stronger, I've made it a point to listen and learn

JENNY:

Only now do you know that the world doesn't owe you a living
Only now can you show that you know how to go on forgiving
I loved you the way you were then and I love you more now
I don't want you to go back again, you would never know how

LENNY:

If I only knew then, I could correct my mistakes
If I could go back again, there'd be far fewer aches
I'd prevent all that pain, and never would complain
Now I've got what it takes

JENNY:

If you could go back again, would you take me with you
Well I will tell you my friend, I would never want to
Don't you ever forget, you're still the fella that I met
I don't want anyone new

(At the reception, Miss Matilda, regarding the tact that Lisa and Bruno are going to have twins, recants (somewhat) her previous advice about dating G.I.s)

BE CAREFUL

MISS MATILDA:

Don't ever take advice if it's not true
If you love each other, little ones accrue
When you're older and much wiser
You can be the supervisor
And can say "do what I say, not what I do"

LISA:

When I thought that it was time to tie the knot
I just chased my man 'til I was truly caught
He captured me when I was hot
And reluctant I was not
He once said two of a kind beats just one tot

(Lenny and Jenny acknowledge the meaning of true friendship with all their comrades)

THE BEST TREASURE EVER

LENNY & JENNY:

Of all the world's wondrous things
Were there any for me
I always thought that (Lenny) (Jenny)
Would be plenty for me
What some people never realize
Treasure doesn't come from things that money buys
When you open up your heart
You can start a trend
The best treasure ever
Is the hand of a friend
But I never knew there would be
So many for me

(At the reception, everyone contributes to the spirit of the corps and what it means to be a member of the team)

MEMBER OF THE TEAM MARCH

LENNY:

If it's true to make a team it just takes two

JENNY:

Then just think what two times two can really do

MATILDA:

You will have so many you will have to organize

LISA:

And the more you have the more love multiplies

SQUAD:

You might unite to make a band or form a crew
A group of many often starts with just a few
Then in no time you will have a whole regime
And you'll be a mighty member of the team

SGT LEATHERY:

As a member of the team you will belong

BRUNO:

To a family whose love will make you strong

LENNY:

The more you care and share the more you will achieve

JENNY:

The more you give to them the more you will receive

GEN RESOLUTE:

There are those who only serve themselves in life
They will never know of suffering and strife
You can bet their pretty hands are always clean
And not one of them would make a real Marine

LENNY:

The things that we possess we have inside

JENNY:

The secret of success is known as pride—pride—pride

SGT LEATHERY:

To pull together's all we need—all we need

MATILDA:

When we pull together then we all succeed

ALL:

No one can ever know just what we've got
But we know what we've got is pretty hot
Its ca-ma-ra-de-rie, in-teg-rit-y
Sister and brotherhood and loyalty

We're America—land where freedom sounds
And op-por-tun-it-y abounds
We rise to the top—WE ARE THE CREAM
We are the members—WE ARE THE TEAM

END OF PLAY

ACT ONE

(Bess is the 65-year-old owner and manager of the Truck Stop. Sally is 19, the youngest of all the waitresses. Big Ben is Bess's husband. Little Joe is their son and inheritor and Sally's beau)

WORTH WAITIN' FOR

BESS:

    Our kids have grown—now we're alone

    It seems it's been about a century or more

But still they had a lovin' Dad

And I can tell you that a man like that's worth waitin' for

    The farther away he is, the less I feel we're apart

    My love grows stronger ev'ry day that he's away

    I hold his faded picture right here on my heart

    And ev'ry day I pray he'll soon be home to stay

The farther away he is, the closer I feel to him

Throughout the years I've known he must be runnin' free

I've learned the magic of the things I know appeal to him

And he's learned all those magic trinkets that appeal to me

SALLY:

    He's young and strong—and seldom wrong

    It seems a century 'til he is at my door

    We've got a plan—and he's my man

                       . . .

And I can tell you that a man like that's worth waitin' for
The farther away he is, the more that I seem to care
I've got so many treasures that I can't let go
Of all the little precious moments that we've shared
And all the wondrous things he's done that thrill me so
The farther away he is, the more that I scheme for him
And when I dream of him my heart won't let me be
I get so lonely sometimes I could nearly scream for him
But I would gladly wait for him for all eternity

BESS & SALLY:

And I can tell you that a man like that's worth waitin' for
It's very hard to find a man like that out there
: A man who treats you like his dearest friend and more
A man who waits for love is very rare
But he could get lost out there and that's my one concern
And sometimes we got troubles knockin' at the door
But when he's on his way home, he knows every turn
And I can tell you that a man like that's worth waitin' for

TEN TON TRUCKERS

ALL THE TRUCKERS:

   I get a warm and fuzzy feelin' when I'm out there eighteen-
      wheelin'
   And the sky's the only ceilin' I can see
   There is nothin' more appealin' than to hear my wheels a'squealin'
   And to feel the road a'reeling under me

MIKE:

   Got a ten-ton tractor trailer that's a honey
   And I love a load that goes from coast-to-coast
   Rollin' down the road and rollin' in the money
   Here's toast to those who boast they tote the most

JACK:

   Got a ten-ton tractor trailer that's a beauty
   Color T.V., stereo and queen size bed
   And I tell you I don't mind it if some cutie
   Wants to stop off at that rest stop up ahead

DUTCH:

   Got a ten-ton tractor trailer that's a titan
   'Bout a thousand horses underneath the hood
   And so many gears to shift I'm always fightin'
   That my biceps keep a tightenin' up real good

BEN:

> Got a ten-ton tractor trailer that's a bruiser
> And she gets me fifteen gallons to the mile
> I just charge the extra petrol to the user
> And go right on ridin' down the road in style

JOE:

> I don't have a rig right now but not much later
> I will own my own and then I can get hitched
> Be the world's foremost owner-operator
> If my gal or pal don't up and get me ditched

RED:

> I went broke one time because of an embargo
> But I'll tell you why I'm bringin' in the bucks
> Got a two-ton rustin' wrecker but no cargo
> 'Cause I'm busy out there HAULIN' IN YOUR TRUCKS

ALL:

> Oh, there's no hill that is too steep and there's no ditch
>   that is too deep
> And no weather that can keep us off the road
> You just call and we will haul you all—no cargo is too big or small
> WE GUARANTEE DELIVERY OF YOUR LOAD

(The lovable little local hooker, Lily, slinks from table to table. At first, she sings softly, seductively and sensuously—then rocks. Bess is annoyed, but the truckers love it—and her)

QUEEN OF THE FLEET

LILY:

Are you lonely, little king of the road

Is there someone you've been longin' to meet

Are you lookin' for a way to lighten up your load

Then come on and meet the queen of the fleet

(rocks)

If you're fond of fondling somethin' that is really nice

You won't look upon me like a piece of merchandise

I don't need your petty pity or your sage advice

'Cause I've been around this pretty city once or twice

(slowly)

You can't help the feelin' you feel inside

You need someone to help put out the fire

No one will ever know it if you're so satisfied

Or had a touch of paradise for hire

(rocks)

Don't you say I must be matronly or mend my ways

When I make a man feel patronly it really pays

I look into your pretty head and what do I find

I am in there somewhere knowin' I am blowin' your mind

(slowly)

Are you lonely little prince of the street

Is there someone you must be achin' for

Are you dyin' for a lover who is so discreet

I'll be your princess and a whole lot more

(rocks) I'm so good at it when you've had it you will know
The queen herself has shown a little king how to crow
Headin' down the road, I'm certain that you will recall
You had her majesty—and SHE'S THE BELL OF THE BALL

(Smokey is the local state highway patrolman. He is handsome, loves him-self, but is not too bright.)

SMOKEY'S THREAT

SMOKEY:

There is nothin' I love more than bustin' trucks
When I pull you over I'm in ecstasy
With my radar on it's just like shootin' ducks
There's no mother trucker can escape from me

Nothin's finer than a hundred dollar fine
I'm in heaven when I'm out there crushin' crime
On a schedule and I put'cha way behind
Then I get 'cha again when ya try to make up time

Gonna get y'all all before my tour is through
On my list of hazards, truckers are the worst
Not a double-clutchin' single one of you
Can avoid it if a drunk don't get you first

And you pay the highest taxes in the state
Maybe that's the reason why you hate me so
Pay my salary that I appreciate
I could use a better bike and radio

(Just before little Joe leaves on the hazardous trip, he and Sally meet in dark corner of the diner)

CRYSTAL BALL

JOE:

I look into my crystal ball and clearly I see

A newly married couple living contentedly

I do believe that's you and me and it was meant to be

And that's not all—in my crystal ball—I see love eternally

SALLY:

Can I see? GEE—look at that!

I look into your crystal ball and clearly I see

A handsome man and soon he'll be returning to me

We're going to be married and live oh so happily

And that's not all—in your crystal ball—I see love eternally

BOTH:

The magic of a crystal ball is what you see inside

It knows all and it tells all—there is nothing you can hide

If you believe with all your heart the vision will appear

You know that it is real because it's very crystal clear

JOE:

I look into my crystal ball and clearly I see

A man and a wife, a happy life, and quite suddenly

I look again and out of heaven soon there will be three
And that's not all—in my crystal ball—I see love eternally

SALLY:

I look into your crystal ball and clearly I see
The sunshine through the window of a tiny nursery
I see your arms around me on our anniversary
And that's not all—in my crystal ball—I see love eternally

BOTH:

The magic of a crystal ball is what you see inside
It knows all and it tells all—and there is nothing you can hide
If you believe with all your heart the vision will appear
You know that it is real because it's very crystal clear

JOE:

I look into my crystal ball and clearly I see
A man and woman growing older so gracefully
I see that we have planted quite a healthy fam'ly tree
And that's not all—in my crystal ball—I see love eternally

SALLY:

I look into your crystal ball and clearly I see
A little girl who somehow has become matronly
I look in there but swear I wouldn't change the scenery
And that's not all—in your crystal ball—I see love eternally

BOTH:

The magic of a crystal ball is what you see inside
It knows all and it tells all—there is nothing you can hide
If you believe with all your heart the vision will appear
You know that it is real because it's very crystal clear

END OF ACT ONE

ACT TWO

(The morning after the bad storm, Ben and Joe are very late coming home from their hazardous cargo run. Everyone is terribly worried. The various waitresses take turns explaining why they would never have a trucker for a husband)

MY HUBBY

WAITRESSES:

If he's at home by 6 o'clock, his dinner's good and hot
If he's not home by 8 o'clock, he better make a call
If he's not home by 10 o'clock, I mean right on the dot
Then he better not come home at all

RUTH:

My hubby is a farmer and he knows the whys and hows
He knows that makin' bacon comes from matin' bears and sows
He gets all hot 'n bothered milkin' cows and pullin' plows
But he feels all warm and fuzzy when he's lovey and aroused

MARY:

My hubby is a welder and knows how to make ends meet
He knows that from a sum of parts he makes just one discreet
When arcin' and a'sparkin' he can hardly stand the heat
But he feels all warm and fuzzy when we meet beneath the sheet

ROSE:

My hubby is a treacher and he knows his A-B-Cs
He knows what courses to avoid and what is sure to please
He's caught a lot of kiddies' colds and every rare disease
But he feels all warm and fuzzy when I sit upon his knees

ANNIE:

My hubby is a plumber and he knows how to expunge
He knows how to use a pipe wrench and the value of a sponge
He knew he was in trouble when he saw that muskie-lunge
But he feels all warm and fuzzy when we take that mighty plunge

JANE:

My hubby has a secret job—to tell I'd be a traitor
He fudges on our income tax—now THAT's an indicator
I'd rather not discuss him now but maybe somewhat later
Aw—what the hell—I'll tell you now—my husband is a WAITER

MARY:

A WAITER! Why, you poor thing.

ROSE:

We never knew.

ANNIE:

You don't have to say anything more.

RUTH:

We won't tell a soul

WAITRESSES:

If he's at home by 6 o'clock, his dinner's good and hot

If he's not home by 8 o'clock, he better make a call

If he's not home by 10 o'clock, I mean right on the dot

Then he better not come home at all

(Sally disagrees with the other waitresses. Her young lover is a proud trucker and she loves him)

A WARM SENSATION

SALLY:

It happens every time I look into his eyes
It happens every time he takes me by the hand
A wondrous feeling deep inside me starts to rise
A warm sensation I can hardly understand
It happens every time I feel his loving touch
It happens every time he whispers in my ear
A wondrous feeling that I seem to want so much
A warm sensation every time that he is near
It's never happened when I've held another man
I've never felt like that with anyone before
Why is it he excites me like no other can
Why is it everyday I want him more and more
It happens every time I taste his loving lips
It happens every time his body presses mine
A wondrous feeling from my toes to finger tips
A warm sensation and it happens every time

(Lily feels remorse about the loss of Ben and Joe. She pours her heart out to the rest of the crew.)

QUEEN FOR A DAY

LILY:

I made all the mistakes that a young girl can
I fell in love with an older man
I can't remember just when it began to
Come all apart at the seams

I only knew that it didn't take long
  Before I knew something had gone wrong
At first I believed that I could be strong
Enough to hold onto my dreams

  I was young and naïve and refused to believe
  That he ever could go away
  It just had to be me I was too blind to see
  I was only his queen for a day
    And that's what made me this way
He collected young dolls with whom he just toyed
He was one of the boys—and the kind that enjoyed
Making fools of his playthings and then he destroyed them
  And then he cast them aside
There were many before me and many to come
The younger the better—all were numb
No one should forgive me for being so dumb

      . . .

I could save not even my pride

I was young and so neat and so cute and so sweet
He always let me have my say
But once I was jaded how quickly it faded
I was only his queen for a day
    And that's what made me this way

(Even Smokey feels remorse over the loss of Smokey and Joe. He hangs up the telephone and tells everyone that he has some bad news. He finally admits he is human.)

SMOKEY'S REGRETS

SMOKEY:

  I often wonder why I took a job like this
  Sometimes I think I can no longer stand the stress
  I should be stout and sturdy and strong and always walk tall
  I have a heart and a soul—and though it don't show
  I know tenderness
And at times like this, I have no courage at all

    I always wanted to make it a little bit safer somewhere
    I always wanted to make it a little more peaceful out there
    I always wanted to do my job better than anyone could
    But at times like this, I wish somebody else would

  I often wonder why I took a job like this
  Sometimes I think I'm really rather something small
  Must hold up—not fold up—under duress and distress
  I have compassion and care and though it don't show
  I know emptiness
  And at times like this, I have no courage at all

(Bess and Sally are distraught over the loss of their loved ones and pour their hearts out.)

A MAN LIKE THAT

BESS:

Are you out there somewhere loadin' and lonely for me

SALLY:

He was so young and strong and men like him are very few

BESS:

Are you waitin', lookin', 'n longin' only for me

SALLY:

Our lives had just begun now we'll never make one of two

BOTH:

And we will tell you that a man like that was worth waitin' for
We never had a notion what the future had in store
We had their total devotion and no man could offer us more
And we will tell you that a man like that was worth waitin' for

WAITRESSES:

A man like you had is oh so special and rare
Can't hardly find one like that out there anywhere
Not one who always showed such tender loving care
Together you and your man made such a lovely pair

BESS & SALLY:

And we will tell you that a man like that was worth waitin' for
He held the only key that ever opened up my door
Now we have lost a life and love that we can't restore
And we will you that a man like that was worth waitin' for

(After the overjoyed crowd settles down, the waitresses and truckers all tease Little Joe and Sally about their upcoming wedding plans and the honeymoon to follow)

MORE THAN THE EYE CAN SEE

ALL:

They look into their crystal ball and clearly they see
That Little Joe is safely home but that's history
They're going to have their wedding day and start a family
But that's not all—in their crystal ball—just possibly
Incredibly—there just might be—more than the eye can see

TRUCKERS:

- He's goin' on a honeymoon in just a day or two
  He'll likely sing a different tune when all the bills are due
  He's got to pay those IOUs—no night out with the boys
  The baby needs a pair of shoes and one or two new toys

ALL:

They look into their crystal ball and clearly they see
A goodwill kiss and maybe just a touch of jealousy
They see the best of wishes from the whole community
But that's not all—in their crystal ball—just possibly
Incredibly—there just might be—more than the eye can see

WAITRESSES:

She's goin' on a honeymoon in just a day or two
She'll likely sing a different tune when little ones accrue

He'll be headin' out for High Rise when all the kids are wet
She's heard his wheels a'squealin' but she ain't heard nothin' yet

ALL:

They look into their crystal ball and clearly they see
A couple facin' and embracin' so romantic'ly
They're sure that it will go on and for all eternity
But that's not all—in their crystal ball—just possibly
Incredibly—there just might be—more than the eye can see
They're gem' on a honeymoon in just a day or two
The awful truth is soon they'll have a different point of view
She's gonna have a let-down—and it's not her negligee
It's when he buys a flannel gown—INSTEAD OF LINGEREE

(Ben and Bess can now retire. Little Joe will own the rig. It's a very happy occasion)

THAT'S WHAT WE CALL LOVE

BESS:

    We're in the twilight of our days
    And in the autumn of our years
    But we have learned so many ways
    To see the sunshine through the tears

BEN:

    And when the winter night was cold
    It seems we always found a way
    To find a little light to hold
    Up high and brighten up the day

BOTH:

    That's what we call love—that's what we call faith and trust
    And sharing and caring and coping
    That's what we call love—that's what we call strength and truth
    And living and giving and hoping
    That's what we call love
    That's what we call love

BESS:

    As the starlight begins to fade
    At last you always will be near
    No longer will I be afraid

Or cry because you weren't here

BEN:

I've never been tempted to stray
My Bess was home waitin' for me
I counted miles day by day
'Til I got tired of runnin' free

BOTH:

That's what we call love—that's what we call faith and trust
And sharing and caring and coping
That's what we call love—that's what we call strength and truth
And living and giving and hoping
That's what we call love
That's what we call love

END OF PLAY

ACT ONE
SCENE ONE

[A dense woods in the middle of the night To the right side, in a small clearing, there is an old-fashioned mountaineer's still. There is a soft glow from a small fire near (but not under) the still. Asa and Ira McDaniels, clad as usual in faded and torn bib-overalls and old, slouchy brimmed felt hats are allegedly "on guard" but are actually lying lazily next to the still, half asleep (Asa and Ira are baritones.)

Suddenly, from the vicinity of the woods on the left side, five very loud shots ring out, very deliberately spaced exactly one second apart In total panic, the terrified Asa and Ira jump crazily up and dance all about on their bare feet They fire their rifles haphazardly in all directions, nearly killing each other. After about a dozen shots, Asa and Ira pause to stare about suspiciously.

From off-stage (deep in the woods) obviously delighted with his prank, Pa McBeam's teasing, mocking voice sings, "Ah Shoulda Bin A Revenoor" (Pa McBeam is a bass.)]

AH SHOULDA BIN A REVENOOR

PA McBEAM:
    Ah shoulda bin a revenoor

    Ah'd got me two dumb mules fer sure

    A piece 'o wahr

    'N 'n old tin can

    Ain't never gonna ketch a mountain man

    Yer 'larmin' plan wahr done by an amateur

Ah got a message fer yore old man
'N all them bastards 'o the 'Daniels clan
Thar's only room
Fer a single still
You got no raht t'be
On mah hill
Ah'm stakin' claim to the spot that whar you stan
Ah shoulda bin a revenoor
Be lots few-er horse man-ure
Ha ha hee hee hee
Hee hee hee hee hee hee hee

(Pa McDaniels arrives at the still and is furious with Asa and Ira. Of course, he despises Pa McBeam. However, he admits no one signs his name with an "X" as perfectly as Pa McBeam)

DAMN MCBEAM 'N DAMN MAH BOYS

PA McDANIELS:

Damn 'n damn to all tarnation
What wer all thet noise

ASA & IRA:

Twar the revenoors ut dun it, Pa
They nearly kilt yer boys
Twar un army trahd to harm us
Snuck up on us Pa, jest lak the cowards wud
But we fought 'em off 'n did real good

PA McDANIELS:
(Examining the still)
Ma McDaniels, from yer innards
—tetched in the haid
One 'r useless—one 'r wuthless
Both'd be better off daid
(Forces Asa & Ira to look at the bullet holes)

Look you bastards; whut you dun
No revenoor shoots that clean
Ole McBeam's been havin' fun
Pertiest "X" ah ever seen
Thet's the onliest way he knows to sahn his name

Even in the darkest dark
He fars his gun 'n leaves his mark
'N puts ar whole damn clan to rot'n shame
Cur-sed, cur-sed, righteous man
Did'nt wait 'til the mash wer hot
De-cent, damn you, kindly man
Lor-dy, Lor-dy, what a shot

ASA & IRA:

Pa, he tuck us bah suhprahse
We never even seed his ahs
Don't pound on us any more, Pa
Wer a'ready good 'n sore, Pa
We'uns itchin' to start a war, Pa
We'uns gonna git McBeam fer shore, Pa

ASA:

Slit his throat from ear to ear

ASA & IRA:

Smash his still to smithereens

IRA:

Skin him lak we wud a deer

ASA & IRA:

Hang him in un evergreen

PA McDANIELS:

Shet yer faces, goldurned fools

You ain't got the guts 'r tools
Takes anuther mount'n' man
To win a faht
Quit cher whinin' shet yer face
Ah'lI put ole 'Beam in his place
Takes anuther mount'n' man
To do it raht
 (Pa McDaniels looks closely at the bullet holes)

PA, ASA, & IRA:

 Cuda got 'er when she boils—he's a curse
 Cuda got 'er in the coils—that'd cost
 Cuda got some jugs 'o brew—that's 'worse

PA:

 Cuda got an ass or two—no loss

PA, ASA & IRA:

 Pa McBeam, yer a rahteous man
 But now yore gonna git cher due
 We got the same rahts what you got
 To make a little gut-rot burly brew

PA McDANIELS:

 Lordy, now we know whut caused all the noise
 Damn McBeam 'n damn it—damn mah boys

END OF ACT ONE
Scene One

ACT ONE
Scene Two

(A few hours after McBeam's midnight raid, little Sarah comes out of the cabin to greet the dawn.)

IT'S THE PERTIEST PART O' THE DAY

SARAH:

It's the pertiest part o' the day
The East is aglow and the sun's peepin' through
The grass in the meadow is sparkIin' with dew
The mountains are misty and magic'ly blue
It's the pertiest part o' the day
It's the pertiest part o' the day
The leaves in the trees highland fling in the breeze
The blue birds 'r singin' such sweet melodies
The butterflies frolic as neat as they please
It's the pertiest part o' the day
It's the pertiest part o' the day
The garden grows green in a heavenly scene
The honey bees pick pollen fit for a queen
The critters are stirrin' cuz ah ain't been seen
It's the pertiest part o' the day

 Oh Lukey, are you out there lookin' over me
 See the perty ribbon in mah hair

Ah'm a'wearin' fer you especially
You will never know how much Ah care

Luke, Ah know that yer of another clan
And to love me you would never dare
Still for me thar'll never be anuther man
Even when mah heart tells me beware

It's the pertiest part o' the day
Prayer meetin' down in the dale
Ah'm goin' and Ah know thet Luke 'wouldn't fail
Ah'd love to think ar luv just cud never pale
It's the pertiest part o' the day

(Luke has been spying on his beloved Sarah. He has his own version of what makes the day perty.)

IT'S THE PERTIEST PART O' THE DAY

LUKE:

Ah'm beholden to this golden time o' day

And Ah praise the Lord fer bringin' it mah way

The bounty o' mah county is the best in all the world

But most of all, Ah thank you for a very petty girl

It's the pertiest part of the day

Mah folks 'r asleep when Ah slip out the door

Ah hahd mahself here bah the ole sycamore

Oh Sarah, mah darlin', yer worth waitin' for

It's the pertiest part o' the day

It's the pertiest part o' the day

If Sarah knew Ah was here what wud she say

She wakes up real early and comes out to play

Oh, God, how Ah wish Ah cud take her away

It's the pertiest part o' the day

It's the pertiest part o' the day

Oh, Sarah, mah darlin' how Ah love this hour

Ah've watched you become such a beautiful flower

Ah'd give you the county if Ah had the power

It's the pertiest part o' the day

    Sarah, Ah'm afeerd ar love would be condemned

    You wud not be welcome in mah clan

    Sarah, they're mah kin and Ah am one of them

Sarah, you maht find a better man

Sarah, Ah cud never let them treat you bad
They are not the kahnd that understand
Y'er the only secret love Ah've ever had
Ah cud never hold yer pretty hand

It's the pertiest part o' the day
Tonight at the prayer meetin' she will be there
Oh, Sarah, mah darlin', if only Ah dare
Ah'I snick you a ribbon to wear in yore hair
It's the pertiest part o' the day

(Ma McBeam lovingly scolds Sarah for getting up so early. Still, there is a lot of work to do)

CHORES

MA MCBEAM:

Little Sarah, whah do you git up before the sun
You start singin' little songs before the day's begun
Ah jest know y're playin' round and havin' lots o' fun
Landsakes, child, don't you know the chores are never done

We—got—ta
Cook a crock o' collard greens
Can a dozen quarts o' beans
Pack the sausages in lard
Beat the rug out good 'n hard
Fix the fence down bah the crick
Got tomato plants ta pick
Churn the butter in the churn
Got the feather ticks ta turn
Go and hoe the melon patch
Lord, Ah ain't got tahm ta scratch

We—got—ta
Go and gather in the eggs
Put the cider in the kegs
Put the hay up in the barn
Got a dozen socks ta yarn
Then we got the dirty warsh
Pick about a peck o' squarsh

Fill the lamps with kerosene
Scrub the floor until it's clean
Then we gotta haul in logs
Till it's tahm to slop the hogs
And—soon—yore

Pa will come down from the hill
Tard from fahrin' up his still
If the house ain't good 'n clean
Then yore Pa gits good 'n mean
He will want his breakfast hot
Then he'll mess with me a lot
If he's had a sip or two
Ain't no tellin' what he'll do
Ah don't feel Iahk gittin' beat
Lahk a bloody hunk o' meat
Little Sarah, ever naht Ah pray thet you will see
A better lahf than what Jehovah dun saw fit fer me
Lord, fer all mah young'un's Ah'll keep pullin' at the oars
Landsakes, child, we jest got ta git on with the chores
Little Sarah, we'uns got a ton o' work to do
You kin do yore singin' missy, when the chores're through
When we do ar hymns tonaht, then you kin sing real loud
You sound Iahk a little bird and that shore makes Ma proud

(Pa approaches the McBeam cabin from the woods. He is in a good mood. Luke has disappeared)

IT'S THE PERTIEST PART O' THE DAY

PA McBEAM:

Ha ha ha hee hee hee

Hee Hee hee hee hee hee hee

Tot them fools a less'n 'n they larnt it good

Now they seen mah mark 'n knows ah mean it

Cud'a killed 'em clean 'n quick thar whar they stood

Now they knows ah mean it cuz they seen it

It's the pertiest part o' the day

The still's been a'perkin' 'n puttin' out dew

In all o' the county Ah'm one of the few

Who knows how to brew sech a beautiful brew

It's the pertiest part o' the day

It's the pertiest part o' the day

The fahr war a'hoppin' 'n poppin' all naht

Ah'm shore that thar cain't be a pertier saht

Than gallons o' licker aglow in the Iaht

It's the pertiest part o' the day

It's the pertiest part o' the day

The revenue men ar asleep on thar backs

Thar'll never ketch me cuz Ah never relax

They jest git all het up cuz Ah don't pay tax

It's the pertiest part o' the day

It's the pertiest part o' the day

Mah woman 'n young'ns 'r wakin' up now
That startin' to see bah the sweat o' mah brow
Ah beat 'em 'n feed 'em the best Ah know how
It's the pertiest part o' the day

(Sarah, Ma and Pa each have their own way of greeting the dawn)

IT'S THE PERTIEST PART OF THE DAY

SARAH:

It's the pertiest
part o' the day

MA:

Cook a crock
o' collard greens

PA:

Still's a puttin'
out the dew

SARAH:

It's the pertiest
part o' the day

MA:

Can a dozen
Quarts o' beans

PA:

It's a rare 'n
Special brew

SARAH:

    It's the pertiest
    part o' the day

MA:

    Got the feather
    ticks t' turn

PA:

    Licker glowin'
    in the laht

SARAH:

    It's the pertiest
    part o' the day

MA:

    Cain't fergit
    we got t' warsh

PA:

    Ma 'n young'ns
    stirrin' now

SARAH:

    It's the pertiest
    part o' the day

MA:

>Pick about a
>peck o' squarsh

PA:

>Feed 'em good
>'s Ah know how

SARAH, MA & PA:

>ITS THE PERTIEST PART O' THE DAY

(Asa and Ira are Luke's totally despicable 17-year-old twin brothers, uneducated, uncouth, and bad!)

CARESS THE WEEPIN' WIDAH

ASA:

  'Twar a rotten naht 'n Ah ain't feelin' good

IRA:

  'Twar 'n ugly saht 'n Pa done had his say

ASA:

  Ah'd git that ole man if Pa said Ah cud

IRA:

  Wal, you cain't—so what we gonna do today

ASA:

  Guess Ah'll go and gut a goat
  Maybe Ah'll jest slit its throat

IRA:

  Or shag a sheep

ASA:

  Or shoot a shoat

IRA:

  Or steal a sow

ASA:

Or kill a cow

IRA:

Ah shore know how

ASA & IRA:

Ah am—rat now

ASA & IRA:

When it comes across the crick
It's shore to git all wet
Hope to hell thet it's a McBeam
Fav'rit little pet
If it's on ar target list
Then you kin safely bet
Thar ain't no critter we cain't get
We say that it's arn
If it is on ar land
And if a yeller belly
Wants to take a stand
He's shore to git a bullet
Clean between his ahs
We'll laugh arselves to death thar as he dahs
Then caress the weepin' widah when she crahs

ASA:

If Ah ketch a city man
Ah won't show no pity, man

IRA:

A rev-'n-ure

ASA:

Thar'll be one fewer

IRA:

From Uncle Sam?

ASA:

Don't give a damn

ASA & IRA:

When it comes upon ar land
Then it becomes fair game
And the bastards only got
Thar bloody selves to blame
You kin bet that we ain't got
A stinkin' ounce o' shame
All them thievin' critters
Look to us about the same

ASA:

Mah trigger finger's itchin' to be free

IRA:

Ah feel a killin' feelin' comin' over me

ASA & IRA:

If the animal we bag

Has only got two legs
He'll feel a blade a'burnin' in him when he begs
We'll laugh at him 'n tease him as he sobs and seeps
We'll nick him 'n we'll kick him as he crawls 'n creeps
We'll slit his throat so neatly if he even peeps
Then caress the weepin' widah when she weeps

ASA:

Tonaht thar's a prayer meetin' down in the dale

IRA:

McBeam clan'll be that Ah bet

ASA:

Mah trigger finger's itchin' to be free

IRA:

Ah feel a killin' feelin' comin' over me

ASA:

You think that jest maybe we'll kick us some tail

IRA:

Ain't seen one Ah cudn't whup yet

ASA:

Hey! You seen that Sarah gal a'hangin' about

IRA:

Now thar's a tail that's shore worth prayin' for

ASA:

Sarah, gal, shore as hell, better watch out

ASA & IRA:

Cuz we're rahteous and a whole lot more

Preacher thinks we're rotten to the core

Guess we better git down on ar knees

Pray to Lord forgive us if you please

Mend us

But lend us

Jest send us

What we're on ar knees a'looking for

A one'n only

Little lonely

Horny orn'ry whore

HA HA HA HA

(Asa and Ira are joined by Pa McDaniels and Luke in this tribute to mountaineering)

MOUNTAINEER

PA McDANIELS:

Lord, A'mahty, how Ah fear

Railroad's gittin' awful near

We don't need no railroad here

Prahvateerin'

Profiteerin

Racketeerin'

Not one o' them's a pioneer

Not one o' them's a mountaineer

Thar ain't no railroad man ut's ever milked a cow

Thar ain't no railroad man ut's ever pushed a plow

He cudn't do it even if Ah showed him how

Got nary a use fer a dad-blamed engineer

Cuz Ah'm a God-a'mahty fahtin', bahtin', shootin',

Backy-chewin', cussin', fussin', bahtin', shootin',

Mahty mountaineer

Thar ain't no railroad man ut's ever slopped a hog

Thar ain't no railroad man ut's ever chopped a log

What makes 'em think a mountaineer's a dirty dog

Got nary a use fer a dad-blamed engineer

Cuz Ah'm a God-a'mahty fahtin', hahtin', shootin'

Mahty mountaineer

Thai's a proper time fer sowin'

And a proper time fer growin'
And a proper time fer mowin'
And a haulin' in the grain
Thar's a proper time fer seedin'
And a proper time fer weedin'
And a proper time fer pleadin'
Fer a little drap o' rain
Lord, Amahty, how I fear
Timbermen's a'gittin' near
We don't need no loggers here
        Prahvateerin'
        Profiteerin'
        Racketeerin'
Not one o' them's a pioneer
Not one o' them's mountaineer
Thar ain't no timberman ut's ever sowed a seed
Thar ain't no timberman ut's ever pulled a weed
They wield a saw 'n use the law to steal yer deed
Got nary a use fer a 'clearin' mah I frontier
Cuz Ah'm a God-a'mahty fahtin', bahtin', shootin'
Backy-chewin', cussin', fussin', chug-a-luggin'
Mahty mountaineer
Thar ain't no timberman ut's ever driv a mule
Thar ain't no timberman ut's ever made a stool
What makes 'em think a mountaineer's a dad-blamed fool
Got nary a use fer a'clearin' mah frontier
Cuz Ah'm a God-amahty, fahtin', bahtin', shootin'

Mahty mountaineer
Thar's a proper time fer breedin'
And a proper time fer feedin'
And a proper time fer needin'
Jest a little sittin' down
Thai's a proper time fer shellin'
And a proper time far sellin'
And a proper time fer tellin'
When to take the lambs to town
Lord, A'mahty, how Ah fear
Coal mines a'gittin' near
We don't need no miners here
    Prahvateerin'
    Profiteerin'
    Racketeerin'
Thar ain't no minin' man ut's ever shucked 'n ear
Thar ain't no minin' man ut's ever skinned a deer
They strip ar land 'n not a one o' them cud keer
Got nary a use few miners 'n thet's clear
Cuz Ah'm a God-a'mahty fahtin', bahtin', shootin'
Backy-chewin', cussin', fussin', chug-a-luggin'
Mahty mountaineer
Thai's a proper time fer weddin'
And a proper time fer beddin'
And a proper time fer dreadin'
What's a'hap'nin' to ar land
Lord, Ah oney got a hunert acres

An Ah'm blessed may boys'll soon be grown
How kin Ah split tip a hunert acres, Lord
Twenty-fahv is all they'd git to own
If Ah leave it all to jest mah oldest boy
What'd happen to the other three
Lord, Ah'm on mah knees but Ah kin plainly see
Railroad men
'R loggin' men
'R minin' men
That is whut Ah-m feered they gotta be
'N they ain't never gonna be
A PROPER TIME FER THAT
Oh, Lordy, Lord, help them
'N Lord help me

MOUNTAINEER—(Continued)

LUKE:

Hear you sayin' railroad's comin' near, Pa

ASA:

Hear you sayin' loggers nearly here

IRA:

Hear you sayin' miners diggin' up the earth

LUKE ASA & IRA:

Then kin you tell us what ar land is worth

LUKE:

Hear you sayin' one's a prahvateer, Pa

ASA:

Hear you sayin' one's a profiteer

IRA:

Hear you sayin' racketeers 'r comin' round

LUKE ASA & IRA:

Then kin you tell us how we stand ar ground

LUKE:

Jest what is it ut a prahvateer does

ASA:

What a profiteer does Ah don't know

IRA:

If we gotta be them things, Pa, Ah do swar

LUKE ASA & IRA:

Then we'll be the best damn 'teers 'uts anywhar

PA McDANIELS:

Hold it, damn it, damn it, cain't you see
We gotta bust up all ar family
Cain't you see that way down deep it's killin' me
Even so Ah figure that it's gotta be
Mountaineerin's disappearin'

Tonaht thar's a prayer meetin' down in the dale
Ah'm goin' to prayer meetin'—Ah never fail
The Good Lord'll save us, Ah got no fear
Cuz yer a God a'mahty fahtin', bahtin', shootin',
Backy-chewin', cussin', fussin', chug-a-Iuggin'
SONS OF A MOUNTAINEER

END OF ACT ONE
Scene Two

ACT ONE
SCENE THREE

[The Gandy Dancer Tavern is a traveling tavern that follows the progress of the railroad. The tavern looks very much as one would expect from early western days, sparsely furnished with one long bar and few round tables and crude chairs. It is still early in the evening and Dixie sits alone at one of the tables. Dixie is about 30 years old. She is dressed in a fancy gown of the 1890s era. She wears heavy makeup and is artificially quite beautiful. Dixie is contemplating her past, present and future. (Dixie is an alto or contra with a rather deep voice)]

DIXIE'S LAMENT

DIXIE:

Man is an animal!

The men all call me Dixie

They used to call me Trixie

A dainty name that's easy to recall

Consequence of adolescence

Senseless and defenseless

When I was Trixie damn I knew it all

Of all the mistakes that I've made

Oh yes

I guess

There have been quite a few

Well I fell in love with an older man

So young

So dumb
So unafraid
I never thought
A girl could be bought
Well
She can
And now I know that that is nothing new
God!—He was beautiful!
Big broad shoulders and slender hips
Honey that dripped from lovable lips
A very small waist and god—he was tall
When I was Trixie damn I knew it all
He gave me all the usual things I suppose
Candy, perfume, a beautiful rose
And pretty little pins that I could wear
We laughed a lot
And loved a lot
I never had a care
He used to say I was his living doll
When I was Trixie damn I knew it all
It wasn't very long before he started staying out
No—it was only a month or two—just about
He said he was out having fun with the guys
He always said that
But he smelled of cheap perfume
The kind a little girl
Like me

Buys
He was a collector!

It was his quest
To conquer little girls!

And use and abuse them for fun
Make them queen for a day
And then throw them away
As soon as he found a new one
They were always too dumb
Too naive and too blind to see
They were always too numb
And I believe they were all very much
Just like me

Ha!

I was his private little tart
With a badly broken heart
So now
I've gone public
That's the way
To start
What else could I do?
Where else could I go?
The damage had been done

I didn't have to become a whore
I already had become one
Man is an animal!

All he really wants or ever needs
Is a bed
And to be fed
And to get bred
That's where I come in
I paid the price and I paid my dues
You tell me what I got to lose
I follow the rail and I've got it made
A man wants tail and I want paid
A man don't want to go too far
A man's not looking for a fancy bar
A man wants just what a woman's got
And it's gotta be hot and on the spot

But someday

Ah—someday

I'm going to go where no one knows
And dress up only in the fanciest clothes
And I'll have wine and fineries
And dine in the finest dineries
And have the tastiest of treats

And stay in plushy private suites
Old men will desire me
Women will admire me
What else would you expect?
I can buy their damn respect!

Oh yeah I was his queen for a day
But now I'm going to do things my way
I couldn't get up till I took the fall
When I was Trixie damn I knew it all

Open up the bar!
First one's on the house!

[Most of the customers are hardened railroad men who sport blue-and-white engineers' caps and have bandanas around their necks. The men and several b-girls hurry in to take advantage of Dixie's treat. The dancing girls begin warming up to the gandy dancers. "Before the prayer meetin' tonight," Pa McDaniels has decided that his boys are old enough to "larn" about women. Having just made a big sale of moonshine, Pa has taken Luke and Asa & Ira to the Gandy Dancer Tavern to meet Dixie. Dixie is always a stand-out. Pa, Luke, Asa & Ira enter and take a table. Dixie shoos away a couple of the girls and takes charge.]

DARLIN' DARLIN' DIXIE

DIXIE *[to the McDaniels]*:

Up north I'm known as Trixie
A name that suits me well
But now they call me Dixie
I've become a southern belle

TAVERN MEN:

She's our darlin' darlin' Dixie
Our dear adopted doxy
A gandy dancer's dream
And that ain't all
From Atlanta to Biloxi
When Dixie's feeling foxy
Then our Dixie is the bell of the ball

DIXIE:

I came down on a sleeper
As far as I could go
The line kept getting deeper
And I made a lot of dough
The train just kept on creepin'
The sleeper had a bed
Didn't need the bed for sleepin'
I'm a thousand bucks ahead
[Dixie puts her arm around Pa McDaniels' shoulders]
What have we here?

A mountaineer?

PA McDANIELS:

W-W-Well

Ah'm old man McDaniels

'N these here ar mah boys

This un's Luke

He's mah oldest lad

The fust 'un thet we had

This un's Asa

This un's Ira

These here two 'r twins

They's full 'o piss 'n vinegar

They's bad

Ah'm cursed 'n more

They's the worst

They's rotten to the core—and cain't even pertect: mah still

From mah sworn enemy—someday Ah'll kill 'em—ah will

DIXIE:

So tell me, Pa

You dear old man

What are you looking for

A little fun

For you or son

Or more   the whole damn clan

PA McDANIELS:

    W-W-Well, ma'm

    Ah done heered yer best at what you do

    It's tahm mah boys larned how to be a man

    You gotta larn 'em thet the thing they piss through

    Feels gooder when it's taken out of hand

DIXIE:

    Why, Pa, I do believe I understand

    Let' see

    Where do we begin?

    With a twin?

LUKE:

    Not me!

DIXIE:

    Not you?

    Pretty Luke?

    Devilish handsome man!

    That's truly true

    Mighty mountain man

    Of all the men I've known

    I can guarantee that's quite a few

    I've had the clean and dirtiest

    But Lukey you're the pertiest

    Of all the mountain men I ever knew

ASA:

He's chicken!

IRA:

He's a-feered!

ASA & IRA:

We ain't!

LUKE:

Pa, Ah thank you kindly
But Ah cain't!

PA:

Jest a dad-burned minute, Luke
Shet up Ma! Ira! Ah'm the boss
We ain't even figured out jest yet
What's this little party's gonna cost

DIXIE:

I'll do you for three, Pa
I'll do you for three
Twins'll cost you two apiece
Five's alright with me

PA:

What about Luke?

DIXIE:

Luke. Luke. I'll do him for free

LUKE:

> Ah've never had a woman, ma'm
> Ah'm sure thet you kin see
> But Ah'm in love with a mountain gal
> 'N she's enough fer me

DIXIE:

> No mountain girl could ever please you like I can
> I'll bet your little girl has never known a man
> I know how to reach you
> Lukey, let me teach you
> That's the way its been since time began

PA:

> Son! You got a mountain gal?
> Ah never heered 'o that
> Ah think yer make-believin'
> Don't even think 'o leavin'
> Tell me whar yer mountain gal 'r at

ASA:

> Lukey's jest a'trickin,' Pa

IRA:

> He's a little chicken, Pa

ASA:

> Ah'm all ready fer mah lesson

IRA:

Ah'm all set to start undressin'

ASA:

Ah kin feel mah thing a' thick'nun up

IRA:

Ah'm all ready fer the stick'num up

ASA & IRA:

Give Miss Dixie the dough, Pa
We 'uns rarin' to go, Pa

DIXIE:

Lukey! Look me in the eye
Tell me what you see
Tell me honestly
You don't want me for free!

LUKE:

Ah see a very perty woman
'N Ah think she's perty nice
But Ah don't need no perty woman
Even fer the price

DIXIE:

Nobody's ever turned me down
Or turned me on like you
I'm going to get your body, Luke

If it's the last thing that I do

LUKE:

Ah'm sorry ma'm
You ain't fer me

DIXIE:

Ve-ry tem-po-rar-il-y

PA:

Thunder 'n tarnation!
Miss Dixie, ma'm
Ah'm givin' you four dollars—lak rat now
Take the twins 'n show 'em how
Ah'm too durn old 'n full 'o gin
Ain't no need to count me in

DIXIE:

Asa, Ira—if I may

ASA & IRA:

Both of us? How can that be?

DIXIE:

It'll be more fun that way

ASA & IRA:

Glory be! Glory be!

[Dixie puts her arms around each of the giggling twins and "escorts" them offstage. Pa is quite amused and laughs to himself—hee, hee, hee. As soon

as the twins are out of sight, Luke makes a bolt for the door and exits. The
gandy dancers notice and carry on.]

TAVERN MEN:

She's our darlin' darlin' Dixie

Our dear adopted doxy

A gandy dancer's dream

And that ain't all

From Atlanta to Biloxi

When Dixie's feeling foxy

Then our Dixie is the bell of the ball

[Immediately after this reprise, Dixie returns with her arms around the
twins. The twins seem very embarrassed. They are busy buttoning up their
overalls.]

PA McDANIELS:

Ah never seen a quicker trick

In all mah dad-burned lahf

Except the tahm Ah give a lick

The naht ah met mah wahf

DIXIE:

Seen cocked pistols

Go off fast but I am not to blame

All I did was touch their crotch

It was ready-fire-aim

Boys are like a raging bull

Sorry if their pants got wet

Since I have been paid in full

That's all they're going to get

ASA & IRA:

You gonna take that, Pa
We didn't larn a thing
You didn't git yer money's worth
We want another fling

TAVERN MEN:

She's our darlin' darlin' Dixie
Our dear adopted doxy
A gandy dancer's dream
And that ain't all
From Atlanta to Biloxi
When Dixie's feeling foxy
Then our Dixie is the bell of the ball
And as they say down south
Your boys got a great big mouth
Get out of here right now or we'll kill y'all

END OF ACT ONE
Scene Three

ACT ONE
SCENE FOUR

[The chapel, like all local buildings, is very primitive. The pulpit, at the rear of the stage, faces the audience. A raised platform behind the pulpit allows the preacher to rise above it and face his congregation. There are no seats of any kind. Distrusting each other immensely, the clans stand to either side of the chapel and face each other.]

PRAYER MEETIN'

PREACHER:

Praise the Lord!

CONGREGATION:

Amen! Amen!

PREACHER:

Hallelujah, brothers 'n sisters
You gotta change yore ways
Satan's waitin' round the corner
Satan's countin' out the days
Countin' out the days o' sinners
Waitin' fer you since you fell
Fire 'n brimstone gonna burn you
You're all bound to burn in hell

CONGREGATION:

Hallelujah, righteous, righteous
Ah kin see! Ah kin see!
Hallelujah, righteous, righteous
Glory be—come to me.

Hallelujah, righteous, righteous
Praise the Lord 'n you'll be saved
Hallelujah, righteous, righteous
If you ain't up 'n misbehaved

PREACHER:

You fell out 'o God's good graces
Ah cud use a hock o' ham
Ah see sinnin' in yore faces
And Ah need a leg o' lamb
You been out thar makin' licker
Ah see sinnin' every day
You will go to hell lots quicker
Less you warsh yore sins away

CONGREGATION:

Hallelujah, righteous, righteous
Ah kin see! Ah kin see!
Hallelujah, righteous, righteous
Glory be—come to me
Hallelujah, righteous, righteous
Praise the Lord 'n you'll be saved

Hallelujah, righteous, righteous
If you ain't up 'n misbehaved

PREACHER:

You been breakin' them commandments
Love thy neighbor as thyself
It's the truth God loves a poor man
Ah cud use some corn myself
You been covetin' yore neighbor
You been gazin' at his wife
If you wanna see yore Savior
Better lead a righteous life

CONGREGATION:

Hallelujah, righteous, righteous
Ah kin see! Ah kin see!
Hallelujah, righteous, righteous
Glory be—come to me
Hallelujah, righteous, righteous
Praise the Lord 'n you'll be saved
Hallelujah, righteous, righteous
If you ain't up 'n misbehaved

PREACHER:

When you sin you pay the wages
You ain't paid mah wages yet
If you want to get to heaven
Ah need all thet Ah kin get

You make perty good white lightnin'
Perty good old mountain dew
Hallelujah, all you brothers
Ah cud use a pint or two

CONGREGATION:

Hallelujah, righteous, righteous
Ah kin see! Ah kin see!
Hallelujah, righteous, righteous
Glory be—come to me
Hallelujah, righteous, righteous
Praise the Lord 'n you'll be saved
Hallelujah, righteous, righteous
If you ain't up 'n misbehaved
Hallelujah, pay the preacher
Satan's comin' after you
Hallelujah, pay the preacher
Little lamb 'n ham 'n dew
Little lamb—'n ham—'n dew

PA McDANIELS:

Hallelujah, pay the preacher
Preacher Ah swar thet Ah will
Soon's a wick-ed sinner
Stops 'a shootin' up mah still

PA McBEAM:

Hallelujah, pay the preacher

Preacher Ah swar thet Ah will

Soon's a wick-ed sinner

Gits his still off o' mah hill

[The congregation is getting very restless. The clans begin pointing fingers and making threatening postures toward each other. The singing intensifies as the clans try to out-shout each other]

CONGREGATION:

Hallelujah, pay the preacher

Satan's comin' after you

Hallelujah, pay the preacher

Little lamb 'n ham 'n dew

Little lamb 'n ham 'n dew

[The meeting degenerates into a brawl between the clans. Luke does not join in but shelters and protects Sarah. The Preacher retrieves a pistol from behind the pulpit and fires a single shot into the air. Everyone is frozen. At that moment, Dixie enters the chapel and strolls straight up to the pulpit. The clans rapidly recover. They are stunned over this sinful intrusion. The Preacher is astonished.]

A PARA-DOXY

PREACHER:

You fell out o' God's good graces
Painted woman o' the night
Have you come here to disgrace us
Or you come to see the light?

DIXIE:

Forgive me Lord—if it's not too late
All my life I've been enslaved
Here's a hundred for your plate
I'm just dying to be saved

PREACHER:

Good Lord! A hundred dollar bill
All your sins are warshed away
Ah jest know thet it's His will
As of now—this very day
Hallelujah!

[Dixie turns about. She has a sweet smile on her face. She strolls back down the aisle toward the door of the chapel. Her head is held high and she nods to the clans. As Dixie slowly makes her way toward the exit, the disbelieving clans sing a very much subdued final chorus]

CONGREGATION:

Hallelujah, righteous, righteous
Praise the Lord 'n you'll be saved

Hallelujah, righteous, righteous

If you ain't up and misbehaved

[Just before Dixie reaches the door, she spies Luke hovering over Sarah. Now, Dixie's true mission is revealed. Feigning surprise, Dixie approaches Luke and leans up against him. Luke is acutely embarrassed but cannot get away. Sarah is totally dismayed. The clans gaze on in quiet disbelief]

DIXIE:

Why my darling, darling Lukey

Haven't seen you for a spell

Where have you been hiding, Lukey

Aren't you feeling well?

Luke, you know that I'm there for you

Luke, you know that I adore you

Who's that little wren?

Hiding in your nest

Looking like she's been rejected

Looking like she needs protected

But then

You know I'm the very best

So come around again

Real soon

Dear boy

Dear Luke

[Now Dixie breaks away and as she exits, casts a longing look over her shoulder at Luke. Sarah is dumbfounded. With an open mouth, she stares back and forth between Dixie and Luke.]

DIXIE:

Bye bye, Luke

See you soon

[Pa McDaniel and Pa McBeam now realize Luke and Sarah's relationship for the first time. They hasten to break up the loving couple. Luke and Sarah gaze longingly in each other's eyes as they are dragged away— back to their own clan. The clans and the preacher leave the chapel.]

END OF ACT ONE
Scene Four

ACT ONE
Scene Five

THE RENDEVOUS

[It is dark outside the cabin area. Luke and Sarah meet clandestinely near the old sycamore tree. At first, they hold each other closely but suddenly Sarah pushes Luke away. She wants to know all about Dixie and Luke's relationship.]

SARAH:

Luke! You tell me when and how!

Thet perty painted woman seems to know you so well

Luke! You tell me here and now!

Ah'm & listen'n really good 'n you better tell

LUKE:

Hush!

Hush! Sarah—dear—they'll hear us.

Sweet Sarah, Ah swear thet Ah don't know her at all

Wha she carried on like thet Ah swear Ah jest cain't tell

'N Sarah, dear, Ah swear as best thet Ah kin recall

Only tahm Ah ever met her, Alt jest run lahk hell

You jest gotta believe me Sarah, what Ah say is true

Ah would never deceive you Sarah, Ah love only you

SARAH:

Jest whar was it thet you met her?

LUKE:

Pa's the one to blame

SARAH:

Jest whar was it thet you met her?

LUKE:

Ah barely know her name

SARAH:

She knows yourn

LUKE:

Ah was only curious

SARAH:

Ah'm a'gittin' furious

LUKE:

At the dad-burned tavern, if you must!

SARAH:

That awful, awful place o' sin 'n lust?

LUKE:

Once Ah seen it—had no need to stay

SARAH:

So you say you up 'n run away?

LUKE:

That's the truth—Sarah—Ah swear

Ain't no woman ever had me yet

Ah bin savin' all my love fer you—mah Sarah

Never been a cause fer you to fret

[Sarah believes that Luke is telling the truth. Once again they embrace tenderly]

SARAH:

Oh dear Luke Ah swear to God above

You're the only one Ah'll ever love

But mah heart is full o' fear

What if mah Pa found us here

Or yourn?

They's the thing Ah'm sick 'n worried of

LUKE:

Wha cain't they jest let us be?

WHA CAIN'T THEY LET US BE

LUKE:

   Wha cain't they calmly let us be

   Wha cain't they simply set us free

   Wha cain't they open up their eyes and see ar love is really real

   Wha cain't they calmly let us go

   Wha do they want to hurt us so

   Wha cain't they open up their hearts and see just how we feel

LUKE *[to Sarah]*:

   Mah love fer you will never dah

   No matter how hard they all trah

   Ah'll never let them keep us very far apart

   Wha ar they always on the slab

   Why do they keep a watchful ah

   Mah love fer you is true and more it's here inside mah heart

SARAH:

   Wha cain't they leave us all alone

   Wha ar their hearts made out o' stone

   Wha cain't they trah to understand and know ar love'll stay

   Wha cain't they calmly turn their haid

   Wha do they want each other daid

   Wha cain't they put away the fear and cast the hate away

SARAH *[to Luke]*:

Mah love fer you will never dah

And they will never know jest whah

Ah'll never let them keep me on the fam'ly string

What cain't they let us say goodbah

Wha do they lahk to see me crah

Mah love fer you is true and more it is mah ev'ry thing

LUKE and SARAH:

Let us hold each other no matter what they would dare

Let us hope and pray thet they will not really care:

Way down deep Ah'm afeerd thet we are not like the rest

Ar love is just the sort of thing they they all do detest

LUKE *[to Sarah]*:

Wha they want to harm us

SARAH: *[to Luke]*:

Don't let them alarm us

LUKE and SARAH

Let us hold each other jest a little whal longer

[to each other]:

Let us hope and pray ar love has jest begun

Let us trust in love and love will make us stronger

Let us love each other and let ar love be one

Hold me close to you

What ar we gonna do

What ar we gonna do

END OF ACT ONE

ACT TWO
SCENE ONE

[It is early in the morning Pa McDaniels is admiring the new outside toilet which he has stolen from the railroad and placed in proximity to the McDaniels cabin. He calls to Ma, Luke, Asa and Ira to come see the new addition. Pa leads off with the song "The New Privy" with Asa and Ira happily joining in. In the same song, Ma and Luke admonish Pa for stealing Pa tells them to shut up and decides to make pfor his transgression by promising to take Ma to the hoe-down]

THE NEW PRIVY

PA McDANIELS:

Come on out here, Ira, Asa! Come on out here, Luke and Ma

Ah has got the pertiest thing here you have ever saw

Stole it from the railroad in the middle of the night

Now jest lay yore eyes upon 'er, what a perty sight

MA McDANIELS:

Whar'd you git that perty privy, it's so big and bright

Got no cracks that Ah kin see, and it's all painted white

Got a moon upon the door so you kin have some light

Ah won't feel the wind no more, them boards look mighty tight

PA McDANIELS:

You all ain't seen nothin' yet, jest look inside the door

Got a brand new catalogue a'layin' on the floor

Folks'll come from all around to see what we'uns got
Best damn outhouse in the county found on any lot

ASA:

Shingles shore are fancy, Pa

IRA:

They ain't made o' wood

PA McDANIELS:

Nope, Ah stole a new two-holer, best 'un thet An cud

MA McDANIELS:

A two-holer! Well, Ah never! Ain't that somethin' nice

PA McDANIELS:

Yep, the best part of it all is we kin fill 'er twice

MA McDANIELS:

Sure will be nice in the winter, Pa

PA McDANIELS:

You won't never git a splinter, Ma

MA McDANIELS:

Has she got a sturdy inside lock

PA MeDANIELS:

Aw, Ma, all you gotta do is knock

PA McDANIELS:

> Lukey, ain't heerd nothin' yet from you
> Ain't you happy Ma's got somethin' new
> It's the only thing she's ever had
> Why you standin' thar 'n lookin' bad

LUKE:

> Pa, Ah'm feelin' poorly cuz you stole
> Sinnin' ain't no way to save yore soul
> Even if you got it from the railroad track
> Ah'm a'thinkin' thet you oughta take it back

ASA:

> Listen to ar brother, Ira, he's the oldest son

IRA:

> Holier than ar new privy, he's a holy one

ASA:

> It's the only decent buildin' in the neighborhood

IRA:

> It cain't be a'sinnin' if it makes ar Ma feel good

MA McDANIELS:

> All mah life Ah made my dresses outta flour sacks
> Scrubbed mah fingers right down to the bone
> Never had a secunt whar Ah ever cud relax
> Never had a thing to call mah own

All mah life Ah never asked fer more 'n what Ah. got
Even all mah pans were hand me down
Ah ain't never had a thing thet Ah cud say was bought
Cain't remember when Ah been to town
Ah ain't never begged 'r pleaded, Ah ain't never cried
Even when mah young'ns all was born
Ah jest learnt to keep mah feelin's all put up inside
Even when Ah felt all sad 'n worn
Ah ain't never asked fer nuthin', never did complain
Even when mah man got stinkin' drunk
Never hollered when he whupped me, when Ah felt the pain
Ever thing Ah ever had was junk
Lukey's right, Pa, you have sinned, you gotta take it back
We 'uns know the Lord said not to steal
Even though it breaks mah heart to sit in that old shack
You had better know jest how Ah feel

ASA:

Luke! You puke! See what you done. Yore breakin' Mama's heart

IRA:

All yore crap 'n holy talk is tearin' her apart

MA McDANIELS:

Asa! Ira! Shet yer faces, you know Lukey's right
Git a switch across yer britches if you ain't polite

PA McDANIELS:

All right! All right! Heard enuff! Woman, hold yer tongue!

If Ah got a thing to say, its whar we put ar dung!

Ah'm as holy as they come, Ah never stole a dime!

Let's jest say Ah borried it—fer a long long long long time!

Now git yer pertiest dress out Ma

'R Ah'll give you a whup

We'uns headin' fer the hoe-down

Oughta cheer you up

[With this threat, Ma McDaniels covers her head and ears with her arms and scurries away. Pa, Asa and Ira seem to enjoy Ma's retreat. Luke does not]

END OF ACT TWO
Scene One

ACT TWO
SCENE TWO

[The hoe-down takes place in the chapel. The only item of furniture is the pulpit As usual, the clans do not mix. Each takes their place on one side or the other. An uninvited Dixie arrives to gaze at the proceedings from the shadows. The McBeams start the party bragging about their banjo man. The McDaniels retaliate with their mandolin man and the rivalry gets quite intense with each string trying to out-duel the other]

DUELIN' STRINGS

THE McBEAM CLAN:

Billy Joe is a banjo man

Best damn plunker in the whole damn clan

Best damn plunker in the whole damn band

Billy Joe is a banjo man

[Banjo solo—clans dance jig a/o reel?)]

Folks come miles 'n miles away

Jest to hear old Billy 'n his banjo play

Best damn plunker in the whole damn land

Billy Joe is a banjo man

[Continue banjo solo—clans dance]

THE McDANIELS CLAN:

Dandy Dan is a mandolin man

Best damn twanger in the whole damn clan

Best damn twanger in the whole damn band

Dandy Dan is a mandolin man
[Mandolin solo—clans dance]
Folks come from miles 'n miles away
Jest to hear old Dandy 'n his mandolin play
Best damn twanger in the whole damn land
Dandy Dan is a mandolin man
[Continue mandolin solo—clans dance]

THE McBEAM CLAN:

Sackbut Sal is a fid-a-lin' gal
Best damn fiddler in the whole damn dell
Best damn fiddler 'n ya shore kin tell
Sackbut Sal is a fid-a-lin' gal
[Fiddle solo—clans dance]
Folks come from miles 'n miles away
Jest to hear old Sally 'n her fiddle play
Best damn fiddler 'n y'know damn well
Sackbut Sal is a fid-a-lin' gal
[Continue fiddle solo—clans dance]

THE McDANIELS CLAN:

Strummin' Stan is a gee-tar man
Best damn strummer in the whole damn clan
Best damn strummer in the whole damn band
Strummin' Stan is a gee-tar man
[Guitar solo—clans dance]
Folks come from miles 'n miles away
Jest to hear old Stanley 'n his gee-tar play

Best damn strummer 'n you know damn well
Strummin' Stan is a gee-tar man
[Continue guitar solo—clans dance]

THE McBEAM CLAN:
Sackbut Sally 'n Billy Joe!

THE McDANIELS CLAN:
Strummin' Stan 'n Dandy Dan

THE McBEAM CLAN:
Hillbilly Billy! Saddle up Sal!

THE McDANIELS CLAN
Go Stan 'n Dan 'n give 'em holy hell!

DUELIN' STRING QUARTET

[Begin "Dueling Strings." Clans gather around to cheer them on. The competition gets more and more intense until the usual McBeam/McDaniels brawl ensues. As was the case in the Prayer Meeting, Luke shelters and protects Sarah from the melee. Dixie now emerges to complicate things by trying to shelter and protect Luke. And, as usual, the Preacher, now standing behind the pulpit, ends it all with a single shot into the air]

PA McBEAM *[to Sarah]*:

Git yerself away from that there kind o' swine

SARAH:

Pa, have mercy—chase away the other kind

PA McDANIELS:

Luke! You call yerself mah son?

Wha you messin' round with her

Never been a MacBeam woman

Fit enough to walk on earth

Now you take Miss Dixie here

Hunderd dollars to the church

If you gotta mess around

Jest think what she is worth

LUKE:

Pa—have mercy—Pa—'n open up yer mind

Ah love Sarah—And you know thet Dixie's not mah kind

PA McDANIELS:

You what!? Ah'll kill you with mah own bare hands
In all mah lahf Ah cain't imagine nuthin' worse
Ain't never gonna be a mixin' up a'twixt ar clans
Ain't never gonna be thet kind o' curse

PA McBEAM:

You hear thet Sarah! Pa is gonna kill his boy
And Ah agree thet thet would end the curse
Cain't think of nuthin more that Ah'd enjoy
'Cept maybe if Ah up 'n kill him first!

DIXIE:

I agree with Mister McDaniels
There's no reason Lukey's got to die
I'll just hold him right here on my bosom
Think of all the corn that I could buy—could buy
Think of all the corn that I could buy

END OF ACT TWO
Scene Two

ACT TWO
SCENE THREE

SARAH CONFRONTS DIXIE

[Remembering the prayer meeting, Sarah was even more alarmed that the uninvited guest Dixie exhibited such an interest in Luke at the hoe-down. Sarah now sees Dixie as a real threat and bravely goes to confront Dixie in a very dangerous place—the Gandy Dancer Tavern. The chapel was Sarah's territory but this is Dixie's turf. They challenge each other in the duet "Sarah's Plea." Frightened by the approach of the railroad men, Sarah fires a warning shot. Sarah backs out of the tavern and Dixie calls the scene that has just happened in "Dixie Reflects." Now Dixie is more determined than ever to get Luke]

[A bewildered little Sarah cautiously enters the tavern. She is carrying a small carpet bag Sarah is immediately approached by a very curious Dixie]

SARAH'S PLEA

DIXIE:

Well, well, well—what have we here?

A little mountain maiden with a ribbon in her hair

SARAH:

Well, well, well—Miss southern belle

An older wiser woman with a perty painted face

DIXIE:

My, my, my—please tell me dear
Why you came to see Miss Dixie—tell me if you dare

SARAH:

Mah, mah, mah—Ah know you well
Wha Ah come to see Miss Dixie—knowin' her disgrace

DIXIE:

Wait!
Don't tell me
What I've always known
You came here to plead with me
To leave your Luke alone

SARAH:

Wait!
Ah'll tell you
What you've always known
Ah come here to plead with you
To leave mah man alone

DIXIE:

Ha!

SARAH:

Ha!

DIXIE:

Look at you!
So dainty and so frail
So tiny and so pale
Lukey is a manly brute and you are such a child
Lukey is a mountain man and really rather wild

SARAH:

Look at you!
So shameful and so bad
So pitiful and sad
Lukey is an upraht man and you are jest a tart
Lukey is a mountain man and rahteous in his heart

DIXIE:

Lukey's got
What makes me hot
And Lukey's just my size
I am going to claim him
I am going to tame him
Luke is going to lie between my thighs

SARAH:

Lukey's got
What you have not
A soul thet's clean and pure
He will never want you
He will ever shun you

Luke is gonna make ar love endure

DIXIE:

Little maiden you don't have the stuff
You're not really rough or tough enough
Little Sarah—go outside and play
Or maybe—I'll just blow you away

SARAH:

So, Miss Dixie—you think Ah am small
Stay raht there cuz you ain't heered it all
Have you ever seed a shrew
Looked into her ahs
You cain't tell what a shrew'll do
Don't depend on sahz

DIXIE:

Why you silly little mountain bitch
Do you call that a threat?

SARAH:

Jest keep to yore kind—painted witch
You ain't seed nuthin' yet

DIXIE:

Railroad men! Come over here!
Meet my little friend
She's dying to meet a gandy dancer
Won't cost you a cent

She's a little virgin, boys
How's that for being rare?
Who is going to be the first?
Who is going to share?

[As the railroad men ominously and slowly approach, Sarah reaches into her small carpet bag and retrieves a pistol. Frightened and nearly in tears, she waves it uncertainly toward the crowd]

SARAH:

Ah've never knowed a man—thet is true
Miss Dixie here knows ever one of you
You better tell
Yore southern belle
Yore pay-day gal
And tell her well
She better never make a play fer Luke!

[The railroad men and a few of the bar girls continue to advance toward Sarah]

RAILROAD MEN & GIRLS:

We've never seen a virgin near a railroad track
Little maiden are you looking for a man?
Once you come this far my darlin'—there's no turning back
There's no mountain man can do you like we can

SARAH *[Waving her pistol back and forth]*:

Y'all keep back—you hear!
Many tahms the only meat ut's on ar table

Is the critter in the woods ut Ah kin get

Any pheasant, squirrel or rabbit that Ah'm able

To fahnd

Wahnds up supper tahm a' bein' et

In the belly

Or the haid

He's jest as daid

Don't you animals do somethin you'll regret

Regret!

Don't you animals do somethin you'll regret

[The railroad men continue their cautious approach toward Sarah]

RAILROAD MEN & GIRLS:

We've never met a virgin that could use a gun

Little maiden would you really shoot a man?

Once you come this far my darlin'—all the rest is fun

Go ahead and pull the trigger—if you can

*[The railroad men move forward a little more quickly now. A very fright-
ened Sarah fires a single shot over their heads. The crowd stops—frozen in
their tracks. Sarah backs out of the exit—still waving the pistol back and
forth]*

DIXIE REFLECTS DIXIE:

Whoo!
So dainty and so frail
So tiny and so pale
She's got a mountain lion's heart inside
But no matter how she tries
Luke is still my size
Sarah, you can say you really tried—tried—tried
I promise you will never be his bride
You can't ever hide him
I will get astride him
I am going to ride him
God! What I'll provide him!

Mountain lions aren't the only ones that pounce
Lukey's got the only gun that really counts
When his gun goes off I'm sure that he'll decide
When I get into his pants
Sarah, you won't have a chance
He will be so satisfied
He will always want a woman
Not a bride
Beguiled
He will always want a woman
Not a child

END OF ACT TWO
Scene Three

180

ACT TWO
Scene Four

SARAH GOT CAUGHT

[Sarah's pet rabbit has gone astray and she is out looking for him. Intent on the search, she does not notice that she has strayed onto McDaniels' territory. The first to notice are the diabolical twins who jump out of the brush. The twins get Sarah between them and there is no escape]

SARAH:

Little rabbit, whar in heaven kin you be

Jest you wait'll Ah git mah hands on you

It ain't raht fer you to run away from me

Ah don't lahk this game o peek–a–boo

[Sarah is shocked as the twins suddenly appear from the brush. Asa stands directly in front of Sarah. He has his hands behind his back Ira stands behind her. There is no escape.]

ASA:

We been huntin' all around

IRA:

In the sky 'n on the ground

ASA:

Now jest look what we'uns found

IRA:

It ain't made a single sound

ASA:

If we shot it—couldn't miss

IRA:

Maybe lookin' fer a place to piss

ASA:

Maybe lookin' fer a thing lahk this!

[Asa jerks Sarah's pet rabbit from behind his back and thrusts it into her face. The little white rabbit is all bloody and hangs limply with head down—obviously quite dead. Sarah covers her mouth with her hands to stifle a horrified shriek The twins are delighted Asa throws the rabbit at Sarah's feet]

ASA & IRA:

Didn't even need the hound
Never far'd a single round
You s'pose 'twar homeward bound
'Spose we oughta knock it down

ASA:

Can it be a little dog

IRA:

Can it be a little hog

ASA:

Can it be a little frog

IRA:

Can it be a polliwog

ASA:

Can it be a little fox

IRA:

Looks to me like goldie-lox

ASA:

Maybe we got ridin' hood

IRA:

What we got looks mighty good

ASA & IRA:

Tell me brother, what has strayed upon ar land
We jest know it's ars cause it ain't got a brand
Only got two legs so it cain't be a boar
Only two o' them whar-as a cow's got four

ASA:

What in hell is it then

IRA:

Brother, we'uns got a hen

ASA & IRA:

Well, if it's a chicken, it's got lost from the flock
Well, if it's a chicken, sure as hell ain't a cock
Never used a bullet
Got arselves a pullet
Cud've knocked 'er over with a rock

ASA & IRA:

Never saw a chicken with a ribbon in her hair
Bet this perty chicken's got some perty underwear
Only way to tell is take a look down under thar
Ah don't 'spect we'll find another ribbon anywhar

SARAH:

Ah'm a'feard o' the game yer playin'
Ah'm a'feard o' the things yer sayin'
Yer sure scarin' me
Ah don't think Ah should be stayin'
Ah'm sure sorry Ah was strayin'
On yer property

ASA & IRA:

Now we got this little chicken, what we gonna do
She ain't old enough to cut up fer a chicken stew
Tell me brother, if we fry 'er what's yer fav'rit part
Ma gives us the gizzard 'n we always git the heart

SARAH:

Ah'm a'feard o' the way yer starin'

Ah'm a'feard o' the deed yer darin'
Yer sure scarin' me
Take yer eyes off the dress Ah'm wearin'
Ah'm so scairt you think o'tearin'
It right off o' me

ASA & IRA:

W'a you perty little chicken, what a good ah'deer
If you peck, we'll wring yer neck and cut you ear to ear
Feed you to a chicken hawk or maybe somethin' worst
Brother, if we cook 'er, ain't we got ta pluck 'er first

SARAH:

Ah'm a'feard o' the way yer grinnin'
Ah'm a'feard o' the way yer sinnin'
Yer sure scarin' me
In this bad game yer beginnin'
Skinnin' me's no way o' winnin
Please let me be

ASA:

Lahk mah drumsticks good 'n tender

IRA:

These 'uns look too dad-blamed slender

ASA:

Tender meat's thar on the breast

IRA:

Downy part's down in the nest

ASA:

Shore cain't git in thar together

IRA:

Ah'm the fust to pluck 'er feather

ASA:

Cain't say, Ira, yer mah twin

IRA:

It's mah duty to begin

ASA:

Yer jest older by a minute

IRA:

That's the law, Ah gits to skin it

ASA:

That's the law, but she ain't clan

IRA:

Ah'm the fust and then you can

SARAH:

Ah'm a'feard o' the pain 'n sorrow

Ah'm a'feard o' the shame tomorrow

Mercy on me

Luke's mah love and he's yer brother
He'll kill one 'n then the other
Just wait 'n see

ASA:

LUKE! You lie! He hates yer guts

IRA:

Little chicken thinks we're nuts

ASA:

Ah'm shore tard o' this here cluckin'

IRA:

Then let's git on with the pluckin'

[As Asa and Ira drag helpless little Sarah into the bushes, we hear The Pertiest Part of the Day in a grim, painful, and very sad reprise. Finally, Asa and Ira emerge from the bushes, still adjusting their clothing]

ASA

Don't believe Ah ever felt so rotten or so good

IRA:

Do believe we stole that little chicky's maidenhood

ASA:

She's a woman now and brother Luke'll shore be proud

IRA:

If he ain't an uncle to a bastard in the crowd

[Asa and Ira depart the scene laughing merrily. Now Sarah, clad only in her torn underslip, crawls painfully out of the bushes and drags herself into the creek. Here she attempts to wash away the sin. Awkwardly, she tries to replace the soiled little ribbon in her tangled hair. Sarah decries her sad situation and the terrible fate that has befallen her.]

SARAH'S CONFESSION

SARAH:

Ah have sinned and thar's no hope fer me
Mah soul will be burnin' forever in hell
Ah'm only fifteen and Ah'LL never git well
If Ah cud jest die now and no one cud tell
Ah have sinned and thar's no hope fer me
Ah have sinned and thar's no hope fer me
Now Lukey won't take me to be his young bride
Thar's no one would have me and no place to hide
Ah'm sick from the shame and Ah'm hurtin' inside
Ah have sinned and thar's no hope fer me
Ah have sinned and thar's no hope fer me
Oh Luke, please forgive me, Ah'm no longer pure
Ah cain't wash the sin away 'n thar's no cure
Ah'll not git to heaven, of that Ah am sure
Ah have sinned and thar's no hope fer me

[Sarah buries her head in her hands and sobs helplessly]

END OF ACT TWO
Scene Four

ACT TWO
Scene Five

[The Gandy Dancer Tavern. The lumberjacks, coal miners and railroad men have gathered for their nightly round of pleasure. The bar girls are artificially beautiful in their heavy make-up and party dresses. There is a lot of frivolous playing around]

THE TAVERN MEN'S SONG

ALL:

We're making this land a mighty nation
Pushing progress is our lot
Bringing this country civilization
Whether they want it or not

RAILROAD MAN:

Drove a thousand spikes today and laid a mile of track
Cleared another mile away and there's no turning back
Tell me miner—logger too—what you got to say
If you didn't have those rails—Who'd haul your loads away?

COAL MINER:

Dug a thousand tons today and loaded forty cars
Did it all with leather hands 'n spades 'n picks 'n bars
Tell me mister railroad man—come on it's your turn
If you didn't have that coal—just what the hell you'd burn?

LOGGER:

Cut a thousand elms today and maybe forty pines

Cleared a hundred acres so you moles could dig more mines

Tell me gandy dancin' man—come give it a try

If you didn't have that wood—how would you make a tie?

BAR GIRLS:

Loggers—miners—railroad men—you say you're pi-o-neers

Got more muscle 'tween your legs than you got 'tween your ears

Tell us how oh mighty men—you'd do all those chores

If you didn't have us girls—your ever lovin'—ladies of the night

ALL THE MEN:

Ladies ?!!!

ALL:

It's hard to be humble when you are as great as we are

The local yokels never could see very far

We're trying to give them all the things that they have not

And by god we'll succeed

They'll get everything they need

And every day—along the way—we'll pray—we don't get shot!

[Now that the twins have become men, they realize just how badly they were cheated by Dixie. To retaliate, they decide to visit the Gandy Dancer Tavern and get their money's worth. Asa and Ira strut to the tavern as if they owned the place. It is a busy time and the tavern has many customers. The twins are approached by two of the regular girls but the twins shoo them away. They spy Dixie seated at her usual table. With an air of contempt and bravado, they swagger up to Dixie]

DIXIE:

Well, well, well—what have we here?

Twin little sons of a mountaineer

ASA:

We ain't little no more

IRA:

Come to see & fav'rite whore

DIXIE:

Well, that's fine if you have money

Might be fun and it might be funny

Knowing you the way I do—I say

Will just take a minute or two—anyway

ASA:

Oh no you don't—you're a'gonna treat us

You ain't the first one thet we ever had

The Beams 's got a whore rat here on earth

IRA:

You owe us 'n you ain't gonna cheat us

We ar mad and sister we ar bad

This time we gonna git ar money's worth

DIXIE:

Careful, careful little boys

I'm not one of your barnyard toys

No pay—no play—get lost

Before you get your little pricks, tossed

Out of here—real fast

On your dicks—or on your ass

ASA:

Hear thet, Ira

IRA:

Ah heerd, Asa

ASA:

Then you know jest what we gotta do

IRA:

Brother Asa you know Ah'm with you

[The twins suddenly flash large bowie knives and point them threateningly at Dixie. Dixie is genuinely frightened She calls out for help from her friends]

DIXIE:

Oh my God! They've gone insane!

Patrick! Michael! Darby! Shane!

[The railroad men rush to Dixie's aid. Asa and Ira turn on the railroaders and slash wildly through the air with their knives. A burly gandy dancer gets between Asa and Ira in an attempt to disarm them. As the twins rush at the gandy dancer, he deftly steps aside. Asa and Ira each plunge their knives into the other's stomach. They stare wildly into each other's eyes as they sink to the floor and die]

END OF ACT TWO
Scene Five

ACT TWO
Scene Six

LUKE VISITS MISS DIXIE

[Three months have passed. Sarah has become a recluse and no longer greets the dawn with her pretty little songs. Luke still looks for Sarah every morning, but she is never there. Luke decides to visit Miss Dixie to get the true story on just how his brothers died. It is early in the evening when Luke goes to the Gandy Dancer Tavern. He enters cautiously and sees Dixie sitting alone at her favorite table. As Luke approaches, Dixie stares open-eyed and smiles broadly]

DIXIE:

Why what do I see with my very own eyes

My beautiful Luke—what a pleasant surprise

LUKE:

Hello thar Miss Dixie—Ah'm feelin' real bad

It seems Ah lost ever thing Ah ever had

Ah buried mah brothers—n nobody come

Ah prayed God forgive 'em fer bein' so dumb

Ah jest couldn't hep it—Ah jest up 'n cried

But Ah still don't know jest how mah brothers died

Since thet tahm mah Sarah—she ain't come out

Kin you tell me lady—what it's all about

Kin you tell me why—'N please tell me true

Ah jest gotta know 'n Ah'm beggin' o' you

Ah'm beggin' Miss Dixie—Ah'm askin' you nice
What kin Ah do Dixie—Ah need yore advice

DIXIE:

Why, Luke—my poor baby my poor little boy
Your brothers died fighting o'er your favorite toy
They both wanted Sarah—Oh yes! She was here
She said she's too good for a poor mountaineer

LUKE:

What are you sayin'—you ain't tellin' true
Ah loved mah brothers 'n Ah love her too
Ah don't believe you so don't say no more
Ah shoulda knowed not to trust 'n old whore

DIXIE:

Ha! You poor baby—I've heard that before
You don't believe me do you dear
I see the outrage on your face
Just ask any man or girl who works here
Anyone in the whole damn place
Tell me Luke—When did you see her last
Seems to me about three months have passed
Ask why she was stupid
Ask why she played cupid
Ask her! Luke, you call yourself a man
Ask her! Luke, just when her sins began
Ask her! Luke, how it could be

Your brothers wanted her and didn't want me
Ask her why she turned them down
Ask her why she came to town
And took a railroad man instead
Ask her why she let a gandy dancer get into her bed
Ask her! Luke!
Why your precious mountain maid
Turned out so wicked and so wild and unafraid
Ask her! Luke!
Ask her if you can
Why she's gonna have the bastard of a railroad man
So fragile and so frail
So pregnant and so pale
I didn't want her kind about
So I just simply threw her out
You just might find her rotting in the county jail

LUKE [now very bitter and unsure]:
Ah'll fahnd her Miss Dixie—If yer tellin' true
What happened to Sarah—Is all cause o' you
Ah'll fahnd her Miss Dixie—wherever she be
You better be lyin'—'r you'll answer to me

DIXIE:
Now, now Lukey
Forget about Sarah
There's no need for you to feel such sorrow
There's no need for you to feel such grief

You and I can leave this place tomorrow
I am all the comfort that you need
I'll dress you in the finest clothes
I'll buy you lots of silken ties
You're so beautiful dear Luke and heaven knows
You can have whatever money buys
God! Those so-called ladies will be jealous
When they see the things that I've accrued
They'll turn green when they've seen
My manly stud
Well I own him and they all can just get screwed
Ha! Don't they wish!
Make love to me Luke
All day and all night
I need those big mountain arms
To hold me tight—tighter—tighter
Love me. Then love me like you've never loved before
Love me Luke until I beg for more and more
Over and over and over and over

LUKE:

Privateerin'
Profiteerin'
Racketeerin'
Railroad buildin'
TImber cuttin'
Co-al minin'
Ever sluttin'

Good fer nuthin'
Whore!

DIXIE [now totally frustrated]:

Man is an animal.
But there's never been an animal that's turned me down.
I'm determined Luke—I'm going to turn you around
You can call me what you like but still
I swear—If I can't have you Luke—no other woman will

LUKE:

Miss Dixie—Ah ain't no animal thet you kin name
You cain't never show me off cuz Ah ain't be tame
Ain't never gonna put me on a leash you hear
Cuz Ah'm a God a'mighty fightin' bite'n shootin'
backy-chewin' cussin' fussin' chug-a-luggin'
Mighty mountaineer
'N so is Sarah!

[Luke departs the tavern leaving a very unfulfilled and frustrated Dixie behind. Only a moment after Luke leaves, the Preacher arrives. He tries hard not to be seen and furtively slinks up to Dixie's table]

DIXIE:

Holy Moses—so to speak—It's the Preacher Man
What in heaven—so to speak—do you want here
Have you only come to call
Or you gonna save us all
Or perhaps you'd like a mug 'a beer?

PREACHER:

Miss Dixie, I done saved you from yer sinnin' ways

A pure and rahghteous lady now you are

You ain't married Ah am sure

Wal, Ah ain't exactly pure

We kin stretch commandments perty far

Miss Dixie, ever since Ah laid mah eyes on you

Ah ain't slept a wink 'n thet is true

Ah am weak 'n made o' flesh

An' Ah got a little cash

Ain't nobody's business what we do

So tell me darlin' Dixie now you know Ah'm lost

All Ah got's thet hunderd dollar bill

Ah got shine 'n Ah got ham

An' Ah got a leg o' lamb

Tell me darlin' what's it's gonna cost

[With a crooked eyebrow and a wicked grin, the Preacher produces the hundred dollar bill and waves it under Dixie's nose]

DIXIE:

Lordy Lord—I do believe I've met a man of God

I see love and charity—unforetold prosperity

You deserve a little touch of spice

Touch of vice

At a decent darlin' Dixie price

Maybe thrice

Preacher man—I'll try to be precise

A hundred dollar bill would suit me very very nice

Since right now I'm pure and free of sin

Seems to me it's time to start again

Oh yes—reverend—I'm the answer to your prayer

You will never get a better bargain

Anywhere

PREACHER:

But—but—don't Ah git any change

DIXIE:

You will feel the change in your heart

And soul

[Miss Dixie deftly plucks the hundred dollar bill from the Preacher's fingers and tucks it into her bosom. She gives the Preacher a seductive "let's go" nod and arm–in–arm they exit. The railroaders and their girls are amused]

RAILROADERS & GIRLS:

She's our darlin' darlin' Dixie

Our dear adopted doxy

A gandy dancer's dream

And that ain't all

From Atlanta to Biloxi

When Dixie's feeling foxy

Then our Dixie is the bell of the ball

END OF ACT TWO
Scene Six

ACT TWO
Scene Seven

[Nearly three months have passed. Sarah is sitting on a log in front of the McBeam cabin, holding her head in her hands. What happened to Sarah has become painfully obvious to Pa McBeam, because Sarah can no longer hide her pregnancy. Pa confronts Sarah and demands to know the father of her child. Because Ira and Asa McDaniels were both involved, Sarah can not truthfully say which one is truly responsible. Pa is so outraged that he will not allow Sarah to finish her explanation. Pa insists that it had to be Luke, Sarah's true love, and Pa vows to shoot Luke on sight]

WHO IS THE FATHER

PA McBEAM *[at first, sympathetically]*:
Little Sarah, little Sarah
Who done this to you

SARAH:
Ah'm not sure which one it was, Pa
Swear Ah'm tellin' true

PA McBEAM:
Ah'm yore Pa, you little girl
Got a right to know

SARAH:
Ah'm not sure which one it was, Pa
Caused the seed to grow

PA McBEAM *[now furious]*

>Why you lie, you little girl
>Sayin' more than one
>You the whore of this here clan
>Fer money or fer fun
>Ah'm a'gonna kill ole Luke
>Fer bringin' us this shame
>Ain't no use to lie fer him
>Ah know that Luke's to blame

SARAH:

>No, no, Pa, Ah swear to God
>Lukey's not the one
>Luke'd never hurt me, Pa
>Please don't git yer gun
>Twar a couple other boys
>Done this awful deed
>Ah'm the one who done the sinnin'
>Beatin's what Ah need

[Now Pa cannot contain his rage. He strikes Sarah hard and she goes down on her knees. Sarah, through her sobs, prays for forgiveness. She begs Pa not to kill Luke]

PA McBEAM *[totally outraged]*:

>If a whuppin's what you want
>A whuppin's what you'll get
>Ah'll beat the truth right outta you
>Ah shore ain't heerd it yet

[Pa strikes Sarah again]

SARAH:

Ah'm tellin' you the truth, Ah swear

Oh, Pa, you must believe

'Twar not Lukey, Pa, Ah swear

Thet caused me to conceive

[Pa now holds Sarah in total contempt. He refuses to believe that Sarah is telling the truth. Pa rudely shoves Sarah away with his foot]

PA McBEAM:

Ah cain't believe a thing you said

Who cud believe a whore

Fergit yer Luke—he's good as dead

You know what Pa's 'er for

Yer a sinner little girl

'N Ah kin plainly tell

You 'n Luke done had yer fun

'N Ah'm a'gonna git mah gun

'N you 'n Luke'll rot in hell

[A furious Pa leaves to carry out his threat. Sarah calls out after Pa, begging him not to do this terrible, unjust deed]

SARAH *[frantically, desperately, praying on her knees]*:

Ah beg you, Pa, please oh please

Ah beg you, Pa, Ah'm on mah knees

Yore gonna kill a rahghteous man

Yore gonna make him dead

Jesus, Ah'm prayin'

Hear what Ah'm sayin'

Oh Lord—take mah lahf instead

Luke—Luke—run 'n hide

It's not yore child Ah have inside

Luke—Luke—git away

Run as fer as you can

Pa's gone crazy in the head

He wants to fill you full o' lead

He's killin' an innocent man

Oh, God, help me

Oh, God, help me

[Sarah now realizes the full horror of what is happening. She jumps up suddenly]

SARAH:

Luke! Luke!

Where are you, Luke!?

Stay where you are

And Ah'll fahnd you

You don't deserve sech 'n awful fate

Dear God!

Oh God! Ah hope Ah'm not too late

[Wiping the tears from her eyes, Sarah runs to find Luke to warn him that Pa is coming]

END OF ACT TWO

Scene Seven

ACT TWO
SCENE EIGHT

[Luke is sitting on the ground near the McDaniels still. He is holding his head in his hands. Luke looks up to the heavens and makes a plea for Sarah]

LUKE AND SARAH—TOGETHER FORVER

LUKE:

Oh Sarah, sweet Sarah—the love of mah lahf

Oh Sarah, sweet Sarah—Ah'll make you mah wahf

Oh Sarah, sweet Sarah—Mah brothers ar gone

Oh Sarah, sweet Sarah—we must carry on

Oh Sarah, sweet Sarah—As God is mah judge

Oh Sarah, sweet Sarah—Ah bear you no grudge

Oh Sarah, sweet Sarah—Mah love is so strong

Oh Sarah, sweet Sarah—You done nuthin' wrong

Oh Sarah, sweet Sarah

[Luke stops abruptly as Sarah comes crashing through the woods and flings herself into Luke's arms]

SARAH:

Luke! Luke!

Listen to me Luke!

Pa is comin' after you

He's all tore up inside

He is gonna kill you, Luke
You gotta run 'n hide
You gotta run 'n hide!

LUKE:

Sarah, sweet Sarah—Ah don't understand
Would yore Pa kill me cuz Ah'm not of his clan
Ain't no other reason thet Ah kin think of
'Cept maybe he's thinkin' because of mah love
Yer havin' a young'n—but he jest don't know
My God! Mah dear Sarah—ain't you told him so
Ain't you told him Sarah—it jest cudn't be
Ain't you told him Sarah—what Dixie told me

SARAH:

What?
Dixie what?
How on earth cud that woman know?
'Twar yer own dear brothers thet caused me to grow

LUKE:

What?
What ar you sayin'
You never went there?
Tell me the truth
Tell me 'n swear
Tell me yer baby ain't one of the clan
Thet you got the seed of a steel drivin' man

SARAH *[begins to cry]*:

Oh yes Ah saw her—thet's perty well known
Ah wanted to tell her—to leave you alone
Whah would she lah to you—whah would she sin
The baby Ah'm growin' is one of yer kin
Oh yes, darlin' Lukey—it's one o' yer clan
Ah never was touched by a steel drivin' man

LUKE *[chokingly]*:

Asa?
Ira?
How could it be
Which one
'N how
'N when
Tell me!

SARAH:

'Twar both!
'Twas the very next day—Oh, Luke—Ah will tell
They got mah pet rabbit—'Twar whaht as the snow
'N then they got me—now Ah'm bound fer hell
Who's the father— Ah told Pa—Ah'll never know
'N now you know what's true
Oh Lukey, it ain't you
But Pa is gonna kill you—even so

LUKE *[Frantically, in tears]*:

Oh Sarah

Mah Angel

You ain't sinned a day in yore lahf

And Ah want you Sarah to be mah dear wahf

We jest gotta git away—Or so Ah fear

We jest gotta git us a long way from here

Ah don't want to be a poor old mountaineer

We'll git on the railroad 'n go anywhere

It don't make no matter as long as you're there

It don't make no matter

[Luke's lament tapers off as he watches Pa McBearn approach. Pa enters the clearing and slowly raises his rifle. Luke shoves Sarah to one side]

PA McBEAM:

Luke McDaniels!—you done messed around

You sinned with mah Sarah—Wha don't you confess

Ah hope you are ready—you won't hear a sound

Mah hill will be better with one Lukey less

LUKE *[frightened but resolved]*:

Ah never did nuthin' wrong Pa

'N Ah'll meet Peter at the gate

'N till mah Sarah comes along

Ah'll jest sit 'n wait

[Pa McBeam aims his rifle at Luke's chest and pulls back the hammer. Just as Pa pulls the trigger, Sarah quickly leaps in front of Luke and puts her arms around his neck. Pa shoots Sarah in her back. Luke has his arms

around Sarah's waist. The bullet which has passed cleanly through Sarah pierces Luke's chest. As Sarah hangs limply there, Luke and Sarah gaze at each other through half-closed eyes. Luke and Sarah sink to the ground Pa drops his rifle, rushes forward and kneels down before the couple. Pa gathers Sarah into his arms and now sees the wound in Luke's chest]

PA McBEAM *[sobbing and looking up toward heaven]*:

God, oh God!—What have Ah did

Oh God! Ah done kilt mah own

Ah kilt two innocent little birds

With a single stone

Have mercy on mah soul—Oh God

Have mercy on mah unrighteous soul

[Pa picks up Sarah, cradles her in his arms, and disappears into the woods. Luke lies dead near the still]

END OF ACT TWO
Scene Eight

ACT TWO
SCENE NINE

[It is dusk. On the little island in the middle of the creek that separates the clans' territory there are three small white crosses placed close to each other. On the McDaniels' side, one cross represents Luke's grave. It is slightly larger than Sarah's which is placed just to the left of Luke's, on the McBeam side. Under one of the cross-pieces of Sarah's cross, there is a tiny one that represents the baby; Ma McDaniels, stooped with years of sorrow and pain, slowly approaches Luke's grave. She has a bouquet of wildflowers in her hand. She kneels down on her knees and places the flowers on Luke's grave. She then removes one of the flowers and carefully places it over on Sarah's grave. Ma McBeam, suffering as Ma McDaniels, slowly approaches Sarah's grave from the opposite side. She has a large pink ribbon in her hand. Ma McBeam ties the ribbon on Sarah's cross and without looking up, slowly takes one long end of the ribbon, reaches over and hands it to Ma McDaniels who ties it to Luke's cross. The dusk turns to darkness as the two old women remain on their knees, staring at the graves of their lost children]

END OF OPERA

CAFETERIA FOOD

BOY ONE:

We have nu-tri-tion ex-perts in our caf-e-te-ri-a

GIRL ONE:

And hy-gien-ists to make sure there is no bac-te-ri-a

BOY TWO:

There's nev-er been a bel-ly ache and no dip-the-ri-a

GIRL TWO:

But when it comes to fla-vor there is no cri-te-ri-a

CHORUS:

Road kill—They call it road kill
Ain't ex-act-ly what you'd call melt in your mouth
Road kill—They call it road kill
Like the north end of a skunk that's headed south

BOY THREE:

They look up all the la-bels and count all the cal-o-ries

GIRL THREE:

They don't a-bide tri-glyc-er-ides nor an-y rare disease

BOY FOUR:

If they just knew that el-mer's glue is not a fix-it-all

GIRL FOUR:

They'd fake it and be not con-cerned a-bout cho-les-ter-ol

CHORUS:

Big mac—we wan-na big mac

Or a wendies or a bur-ger king and fries

Big mac—we wanna big mac

Or a ta-co bell or piz-za hut sur-prise

BOY FIVE:

If they'd pay more at-ten-tion to the fla-vor of the stew

GIRL FIVE:

And less at-ten-tion to the fat-ty a-cids that ac-crue

BOY SIX:

They could form a gour-met for-mu-la for me and you

GIRL SIX:

There is no end to all the rec-I-pes that they could do

CHORUS:

Fast food—We feast on fast food

Tas-ty ta-cos chees-y piz-zas and big macs

Fast food—We feast on fast food

Ev-en though we know we'll all have heart attacks

(FEISTY SENIOR GIRL)

I DON'T NEED A CHAPERONE

I told him—

    Dad-dy, this is gon-na be a ver-y spe-cial dance

    What you're do-in's gon-na ru-in my chance for ro-mance

    I'm not dumb e-nough to give a boy a sec-ond glance

    If I think that he just wants to get in-to my pants

I told him—

    Dad-dy, if you care for me—don't you

                dare em-bar-rass me

    To-night at the prom

    I would ra-ther go a-lone—I don't need a chap-e-rone

    To-night at the prom

I told him—

    Dad-dy, I don't need a cop—I know when

                it's time to stop

    To-night at the prom

    You don't know 'cause you're all grown—

                I don't need a chap-e-rone

    To-night at the prom

I told him—

    Dad-dy, won't you ev-er learn—you don't have to

                take your turn

    To-night at the prom

    I can make it on my own—I don't need a chap-e-rone

    To-night at the prom

HE TOLD ME—

    Tee-ny bop-per daugh-ter you've a mind of your own

    And cer-tain-ly your friends know so much
                    more than I do

    You think you're ra-ther cle-ver and you know
                  you're pret-ty smart

    But what I have to tell you comes sin-cere-ly
                  from my heart

    Dar-lin' I was once a teen—but I've ver-y rare-ly seen

    Some Dads at a prom

    It's be-cause I real-ly care—you can bet you'll see me there
        —I TOOK YOUR MOM TO THE PROM

BEING CHASED AND BEING CHASTE

SOPHOMORES:

Your part-ner at the part-y was a per-fect date
Now the oth-er part-y's start-in' and it's get-tin' late
He's a guy and he will try to get you good and hot
If you want him to re-spect you then you bet-ter not
It will take all the cour-age that you've got

HIGH SCHOOL CHORUS :

Be-ing chased is ex-cit-ing when it's spelled with a "d"
But be-ing chaste is sa-cred when it's spelled with a "t"
The price of runnin' wild
Is an un-want-ed child
And no one wants chil-dren hav-ing chil-dren

JUNIORS:

You could have said good night be-fore he came in the door
But the ten-der kiss he gave you made you want one more
Pret-ty soon you will dis-cov-er what he's look-in' for
Rus-sian hands and rom-an fing-ers eag-er to ex-plore
Re-fuse or lose what you can-not re-store
(CHORUS)

SENIORS:

When you're set-tin' on the set-tee and be-gin to pet
Soon the pet-tin's get-tin' heav-y and you start to sweat
He's a guy who'll try to see how far that he can get

215

You had better tell your bud-dy you ain't read-y yet
In the fu-ture you will have no re-gret
(CHORUS)

FRESHMEN:

We're on-ly fresh-men but we know a-bout psy-chol-o-gy
We're way a-head on soph-more stuff like bi-ol-o-gy
Phys-i-ol-o-gy is some-thin' that should make us whole
But we won-der why it's just not called bod-y and soul
We know that we just got-ta keep con-trol

WRONG STUFF—RIGHT STUFF

BOY-IN BLACK:

Have I got stuff for you!

Come and see me at the rave

I've got ev-'ry-thing you crave

L-S-D 'n ec-sta-sy

Crack co-caine 'n mary jane

Stuff to end your ev-'ry pain

Stuff to pul-ver-ize your brain

Stuff that glori-fies de-scrip-tion

Stuff you can't get by pre-scription

Stuff to put you up on top

Stuff for twen-ty bucks a pop

Think how much you're gon-na save

Come and see me at the rave

GIRL-IN WHITE:

Let me tell you about the right stuff!

Stay a-way from slime like that

He's a push-er—he's a rat

If you see him at the rave

Just say no 'n then be-have

Stuff is cour-age—stuff is dare

Stuff is what it takes to care

Stuff is val-or—stuff is brave

Stuff is what it takes to save

Stuff is guts and pluck and grit
Stuff can make the push-er quit
Think if you can make him go
All you need is just say no

SENIOR CHORUS:

Stu-dent loans and schol-ar-ships are what we dear-ly need
Watch them quick-ly dis-ap-pear if we're caught doing speed
Just one fel-o-ny con-vic-tion—we can't take it back
We will have a re-cord for a lit-tle crack 'r smack
We were be-ing cle-ver—oh we were be-ing hip
Now say good-bye to our stu-dent loan and to our schol-ar-ship
It's not worth it—why we try it—heav-en on-ly knows
The devil made us do it—d'ya sup-pose?

DAD'S APOLOGY

SOPHOMORE BOY:

Sing a song of sixpence, a pocketful of rye
Four-and-twenty blackbirds, baked in a pie
The birdies all were ravens, but how was I to know
That when I had a piece of pie, I was really eating crow

SEWER-SIDE

He lay on his side in the sewer
And there in the sewer he died
The coroner did an autopsy
    And called it sewer-side

THE HAVES AND THE HAVE-NOTS

The haves and the have-nots are somewhat different breeds
The haves have all the affluence the poorer have-not needs
Which one is truly better off is so hard to decide
The have-nots thrive on welfare while the haves do suicide

www.ingramcontent.com/pod-product-compliance
Lightning Source LLC
Chambersburg PA
CBHW021052090426
42738CB00006B/298